FUNDAMENTALS OF ATTITUDE MEASUREMENT

WILEY FOUNDATIONS OF SOCIAL PSYCHOLOGY SERIES

Series Editor: **DANIEL KATZ**, University of Michigan

BOOKS IN THE SERIES

ATTITUDE AND ATTITUDE CHANGE
TRIANDIS, HARRY C., University of Illinois

GROUP PROCESSES
BURNSTEIN, EUGENE, University of Michigan

FUNDAMENTALS OF ATTITUDE MEASUREMENT
DAWES, ROBYN, University of Oregon and Oregon Research Institute

COGNITIVE CONSISTENCY AND COGNITIVE BALANCING
FEATHER, NORMAN, University of New England, Australia
*

SOCIAL ORGANIZATION
GEORGOPOULOS, BASIL, University of Michigan

SOCIAL PERCEPTION
MENDELSOHN, GERALD, University of California, Berkeley

SOCIAL INFLUENCE
MILLER, NORMAN, University of Southern California

SOCIAL MOTIVATION
SMITH, CHARLES, Brooklyn College

Fundamentals of Attitude Measurement

ROBYN M. DAWES

University of Oregon and
Oregon Research Institute

JOHN WILEY & SONS, INC.

NEW YORK · LONDON · SYDNEY · TORONTO

Library of Congress Cataloging in Publication Data

Dawes, Robyn M   1936—
Foundations of attitude measurement.

(Wiley foundations of social psychology series)
Bibliography: p.
1. Attitude (Psychology) 2. Scale analysis
(Psychology) 3. Social psychology--Research.
I. Title.

BF323.C5D38   152.4'52   75-39033
ISBN 0-471-19949-4
ISBN 0-471-19950-8 (pbk.)

Printed in the United States of America.

10 9 8 7 6 5 4 3 2 1

Series Preface

The phenomenal growth of social psychology during the past thirty-five years has occurred both in depth—in the development of its root system of experimental studies—and in breadth—in its branching out to embrace the social realities covered by the more traditional social sciences. In 1935, the first handbook of social psychology (edited by Carl Murchison), even with its many chapters from anthropology and demography, comprised a single volume. In 1969, the second edition of the Lindzey *Handbook* included five volumes. How then can we communicate to the various interested publics the findings and concepts of this far-flung enterprise? The handbooks with their summaries of the literature and their extensive bibliographies fulfill the needs of the specialist, but what about other audiences? The traditional method of a single text for a single course entails great difficulties in communicating the basic knowledge in the field to students or to other interested readers.

In this series we propose an alternative to the traditional methods by providing a number of separate volumes based on the major areas of interest for social-psychological research. Each book, although considerably shorter than a text, permits a more thorough treatment of a subarea than a text chapter. Several of these volumes provide the critical blocks of material for an introductory course, and particular books furnish the basis for an advanced course. The objective is to avoid the single textbook's scanty coverage of important issues and, also, to avoid the handbook type of treatment, which is too detailed and cryptic for the needs of the broader audience. Moreover, reader motivation will improve with the investigation of a single problem area that is broad enough to represent meaningful patterns of relationships and yet sufficiently delimited to permit a depth of study.

Interestingly, the field itself is developing in this direction. Researchers are concentrating their efforts on a related series of problems and are foregoing both grand theory and scattered pieces of empiricism. They are accumulating knowledge through their communication and contact within the given subareas of the field. If findings are to be replicated, if their determinants are to be systematically explored, if they are to be generalized to other settings, then the frame of reference must encompass the relevant work of others in the same vineyeard. Empirical studies show that scientific communication for active researchers takes place along these lines. It is less a matter of systematic perusal of all the journals and more a matter of informal communication among those with common research interests, through the exchange of preprints, letters, and discussion. Although this does not provide for the theoretical integration of all of social psychology, it does lead to the cumulative building of knowledge in a given subarea. This systematic accumulation is a prerequisite for scientific development and for later more comprehensive theory construction.

This series takes advantage of these research developments, especially as they are linked to the continuing problem areas in social psychology. It provides the student, the teacher, and the interested consumer of social science with a systematic account of what is known in fields such as social motivation, attitude structure and change, group processes and interpersonal behavior, social influence, the psychological aspects of social systems, balance theories, interpersonal perception, and attitude measurement. The series permits the instructor to select the areas that he considers of greatest importance for coverage in general and specialized courses in social psychology.

Daniel Katz

University of Michigan

Preface

This book grew out of three beliefs: (1) that attitudes are important—especially in a technologically advanced society in which the attitudes of particular people or groups can have profound (sometimes devastating) effects; (2) that many people will therefore want to understand how attitudes are measured; and (3) that the basic ideas of attitude measurement can be presented in a simple, nontechnical manner which can be understood by readers with little mathematical background. This book makes such a presentation.

This book is primarily a text for undergraduates taking introductory courses in social psychology, attitudes, measurement, or even attitude measurement. It can also be used in more advanced courses as an adjunct textbook for background in the basic concepts of attitude measurement or measurement in general.

Although this book is short, it covers most basic types of attitude measurement; it does not survey the wide variety of actual techniques. However, each type of measurement is illustrated by at least one technique applied to an attitude domain chosen for its intrinsic interest.

Representational measurement techniques are categorized according to a slight modification of Coombs' (1964) classification system. There are four categories covered in Chapters III to VI, which follow an introductory chapter (I) and a chapter disucssing the meaning of "measurement" and "attitude" (II). Chapter VII presents material relevant to representational measurement in general, and Chapters VIII to X describe common types of index measurement. Finally, Chapter XI provides a brief integration of the previous material.

With the exception of Chapters I and XI, each ends with a series of questions meant to stimulate the reader to think about basic issues and problems. These questions involve conceptual issues, not routine computations.

Robyn M. Dawes

Acknowledgments

Whatever virtues this book has are due in large part to the sexist nature of contemporary United States society, which forced three remarkable young women to accept work as my secretary—despite the fact that their talents and abilities qualified them for much more important and lucrative employment. Judy Boylan and Jan Thoele typed flawlessly, corrected grammar, pointed out vague passages (diplomatically), and made many valuable comments. Dixie Frazer, who was with me prior to the actual writing of the book, helped greatly in the work leading up to it.

I am deeply indebted to many friends and colleagues who read the first draft of this book and made excellent substantive and editorial suggestions. They are Robert Abelson, Norman Anderson, Norman Cliff, Clyde Coombs, Lewis Goldberg, Louis Guttman, Daniel Katz, Phillip Runkel, Harry Triandis, Amos Tversky, and Benjamin Winter, who are among today's outstanding figures in the area of psychological measurement. I am fortunate to have had their advice. I did not accept all of their suggestions and, of course, they are not responsible for any of the book's shortcomings.

Paul Hoffman, Lew Goldberg, and Len Rorer were largely responsible for providing the facilities and an atmosphere at the Oregon Research Institute that made working and writing there a joy—just as Robert Fagot and Dick Littman were mainly responsible for providing a similar atmosphere in the psychology department at the University of Oregon. Daniel Katz, editor of this series, was of inestimable help in providing moral support and practical guidance. But perhaps my greatest indebtedness is to my mentor, Clyde Coombs, whose creative ideas and insights provided a basis for much of the book's contents.

Finally, I express gratitude to Carol, my former wife, who—during the occasional periods of drudgery that are inevitable for a writer—helped to keep life interesting and occasionally extremely enjoyable.

The preparation of this book was supported in part by Grant No. MH 12972 from the National Institute of Mental Health, U.S. Public Health Service.

R.M.D.

Contents

FUNDAMENTALS OF ATTITUDE MEASUREMENT

Introductory Chapters

The purpose of this book is explained in Chapter I. In Chapter II, there is a discussion of the nature of "measurement" and of the distinction between *representational measurement* and *index measurement.* Chapter II also presents various definitions of "attitude."

I

Introduction

In 1935 Gordon Allport observed that "attitudes today are measured more successfully than they are defined." This statement is still true in 1971.

It is difficult to define "attitudes," and although attempts to measure attitudes have been more successful than have attempts to define them, it does not follow that attitudes are measured easily. Certainly, they are not as easily measured as they appear to be from assertions of the mass media. The American people have been told, for example, that certain people have racist attitudes (some more than others), that the American public's attitude toward the war in Vietnam shifted radically between 1967 and 1971, and that a vast majority of that public supported President Johnson as he escalated the war—all with the same assurance that they were told that Martin Luther King was black, that there were 530,000 American troops in Vietnam in 1967, and that President Johnson decided not to seek reelection. Attitudes, however, are not often measured as easily as is skin color; they are not always as obvious as undisguised troop movements, nor as public as a speech announcing retirement.

This book attempts to outline exactly *how* attitudes are measured. It will be shown that simply asking a man whether he supports his president or requiring him to put a check mark on a rating scale does not necessarily result in anything's being measured, especially not the man's attitudes. Instead, certain *imperical conditions* must be satisfied if attitude measurement is to occur. The purpose of this book is to explain the nature of these conditions while presenting some of the most common and successful techniques for measuring attitude. Thus, the book is concerned with the logical foundations of attitude measurement; it is not a "cookbook" of methods.

Why should the beginning student be concerned with the logic of attitude measurement instead of with mastering specific techniques? The answer is threefold. First, current attitude measurement techniques are not so good that they should be accepted for their heuristic value alone. We cannot say to a man who is seriously interested in studying racist attitudes, "Look, here is a questionnaire for measuring these attitudes; it will do a good job; don't worry about where it came from." The man must understand something about attitude measurement if he is to evaluate responses to an attitude questionnaire.

A second reason for writing an introductory book on fundamentals is that an increasing number of students today are quite properly rebelling against education consisting of pasta that the teacher believes, which is to be swallowed without question. This book is written in the hope that these students will not be content with rote learning of techniques, but will value—for its own sake—an understanding of these techniques.

A third reason is, frankly, to generate skepticism. As has been indicated, atitudes are often discussed as if they were easily assessed and measured; the result can be sweeping and fallacious beliefs about people's attitudes. Uncritical acceptance of various techniques does not lead to an understanding of which beliefs are reasonable and which are unreasonable.

Many of us social psychologists claim to have good methods for measuring attitudes; if our claim is correct, we should be able to explain to the person who understands the fundamentals of attitude measurement why our methods are good ones. I hope that the student who reads this book will become such a person.

Attitudes Can
Be Measured

2.1 Representational Measurement

This chapter is named after L. L. Thurstone's 1928 revolutionary *American Journal of Sociology* article in which he described a general method for measuring attitudes. In a later article he showed how this method could be applied to measure the seriousness of crimes (more specifically, the seriousness of crimes as judged by students at the University of Chicago).

In order to understand the import of Thurstone's article, it is necessary to have some knowledge of the developments in measurement theory that preceded it, even though those developments were not in the domain of attitude measurement. A brief review follows.

In the latter part of the nineteenth century, several men interested in both psychology (then philosophy) and physics performed experiments meant to elucidate the relationship between the mind (*psyche*) and the external (*physical*) world. Such *psychophysicists* attempted to determine how physical intensity was related to psychological intensity; for example, they tried to ascertain how the physical intensity of light as measured in foot candles is related to its psychological brightness, or how physical intensity of a noise as measured in decibels is related to its psychological loudness.

But how are variables like "psychological brightness" and "psychological loudness" to be measured? The most common method proposed was the *confusion* method, which is based on the assumption that if a subject is forced to make a judgment about which of two stimuli is more intense when both are equally intense psychologically, he will choose each stimulus equally often; if, on the other hand, the stimuli are not equally intense psychologically, he will choose the more intense one with a probability greater than .50, but not always with probability 1.00. The probability with which one stimulus is chosen as more intense than the other is converted to a "psychological distance" between the two stimuli. (This probability is usually estimated from proportions based on independent choices.)

Actually, there are many confusion methods—a different method for each way probability is converted into psychological distance. All these methods rely on confusion between the stimuli, confusion in that the stimuli used are neither perfectly discriminable nor perfectly indiscriminable.

The most common method used was that of the *just noticeable difference.* One stimulus is defined to be just noticeably different from another if it is actually perceived to be more intense than the other with probability .50. The subject must guess which is more intense on trials when he does not actually perceive a difference, and—if the experiment is done well—he will guess each stimulus with equal probability. Hence, a stimulus that is just noticeably more intense than another will be judged to be more intense with probability .75, for with probability .50 the subject perceives a difference, and with probability .25 (= .50 x .50), he does not perceive a difference but guesses correctly. Stimulus *a* is, therefore, *defined* to be just noticeably different from stimulus *b* whenever it is judged to be more intense than *b* with probability .75. These just noticeable differences are often regarded as units in the scale of psychological intensity.

Essentially, what Thurstone proposed in his paper was that the method of confusion could be used in contexts where there is no physical dimension that parallels the psychological dimension under investigation. He argued that although we happen to be able to measure physical intensity of light in terms of foot candles, this ability is in no way essential to our constructing a psychological brightness scale by the method of just noticeable differences. Such a scale could be equally well constructed if we did not have any idea of how to measure the physical intensity of light. Thurstone proposed then that the confusion method, or methods, could be used to measure the psychological intensity of any stimuli; in particular, they could be used to measure the intensity of attitudes on any dimension of interest. For example, the probability that one sample of handwriting is judged to be more aesthetically pleasing than another may be used to locate these two samples on a dimension of aesthetic pleasingness, or the probability that one crime is judged to be more serious than another may be used to locate these two crimes on a dimension of judged seriousness (intensity).

The actual methods Thurstone proposed were not based on just noticeable differences. These methods—which Thurstone referred to as the "laws of comparative judgment"—are based on the assumption that each stimulus does not correspond to a single point on the psychological dimension but instead to a distribution centered around a point; thus, a stimulus will sometimes be perceived to be more intense and sometimes less intense. This assumption is illustrated in Figure 1*a*; here, the probability that an individual perceives the stimulus to lie between points *x* and *y* on the intensity dimension is represented by the proportion of the area under the curve lying between points *x* and *y*.

Now consider two stimuli whose distributions overlap, as illustrated in Figure 1*b*. Suppose also that the distribution representing stimulus *b* is higher on the intensity dimension than is that representing stimulus *a*. When a subject is asked which of these two stimuli is more intense, he is assumed to sample a value from the distribution of *a* and to sample a value from the distribution of *b*. He states that *a* is more intense than *b* whenever his sample from *a*'s distribution is higher than that from *b*'s. Usually the value from *b*'s distribution will be more intense than that from *a*'s distribution, but occasionally the value from *a*'s distribution will be greater, since the distributions overlap. As is intuitively obvious, the more the distributions overlap, the greater the probability that the sample from *a*'s

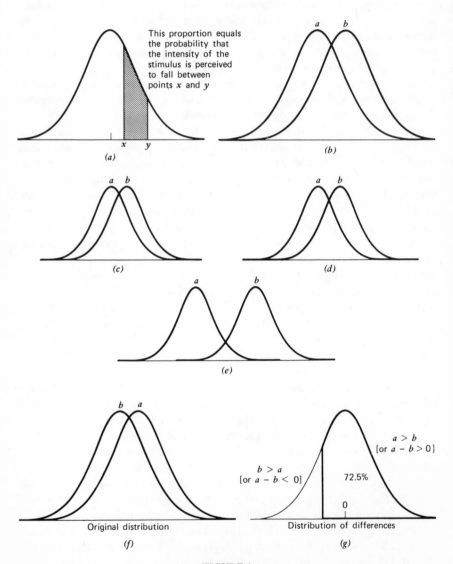

FIGURE 1.

distribution will be more intense than that from *b*'s distribution. Various degrees of overlap are illustrated in Figure 1*c* to 1*e*.

If the shape of the distributions is known and if any correlation between a judge's sampling from *a* and *b* is known, then the probability that he judges *b* to

FIGURE 2.

be more intense than a is determined entirely by the overlap in the distributions of a and b; hence, an estimate of this probability may be used to estimate the extent of this overlap. Thurstone assumed that these distributions were of the type known as normal distributions (i.e., bell shaped); furthermore, in his most common method (referred to as "Case 5"), he assumed that the standard deviations of all these distributions are equal—so that they are shaped as in Figure 1—and that sampling from the two distributions is independent (therefore, uncorrelated). Then, the degree to which the distributions overlap is entirely determined by the distance between their means, and this distance may be easily computed by knowing the probability that b is judged to be more intense than a. The distance between the means of the distributions of a and b is defined as the distance between their *values* on the dimension. The actual method for obtaining the distance between such values involves use of normal curve properties.[1]

In 1927 Thurstone presented pairs of 19 crimes to 266 University of Chicago students and asked the students to pick the member of each pair that was more serious. He took the resulting proportion of people who chose crime a as more serious than crime b as an estimate of the probability that a is judged to be more serious than b by this particular population. Applying the measurement technique outlined here (Case 5 of the law of comparative judgment), he obtained the dimension of judged seriousness presented in the left-hand side of Figure 2; the crimes are shown at the estimated means of their distributions, that is, at their values on the dimension of judged seriousness. (The actual locations are obtained by a procedure of amalgamating distances between values according to a "least squares" criterion.)

The dimension on the right side of Figure 2 illustrates the judged seriousness of crimes for a sample of 369 University of Michigan students in 1966; these data were collected by Coombs (1967), who used the same procedures and technique as did Thurstone 39 years earlier. In comparing these two dimensions, it is of interest to note that sexual crimes (rape, seduction, abortion, and adultery) were judged relatively less serious in 1966 than in 1927, while crimes involving bodily injury (homicide, kidnapping, assault and battery) were judged relatively more serious; specifically, the biggest differences in position on the

---

[1]This method will be outlined briefly for the benefit of the reader familiar with the necessary statistical concepts. Since a and b are independent and are both normally distributed, the distribution of differences between a and b is also normally distributed; the mean of this distribution of differences is equal to the difference between the two means, and its variance is equal to the sum of the variances. The probability that a sample from a is more intense than a sample from b is exactly equal to the probability that a sample from the distribution of differences is greater than zero; hence, this probability gives us the proportion of the distribution of differences that is above zero. From this proportion, the number of standard deviations between the zero point and the mean of the distribution of differences is obtained, which is precisely the difference between the two means measured in terms of the standard deviation of the distribution of differences. Dividing by this standard deviation yields the differences between the means. This method is illustrated in Figure 1f.

dimensions are found for the crimes of abortion, adultery, seduction, and assault and battery—the former three "crimes" being judged to be relatively less serious in 1966, and the last being judged to be relatively more serious. Crimes involving the destruction of property occupy relatively the same position on the dimensions for both years. The differences between the 1927 judgments and the 1966 judgments are not surprising in light of the change in attitudes toward sexual activity and deviation in the intervening years. Finally, notice that the positions of the crimes on the dimensions do not necessarily reflect the severity of sentencing for these crimes; for example, assault and battery is judged to be a

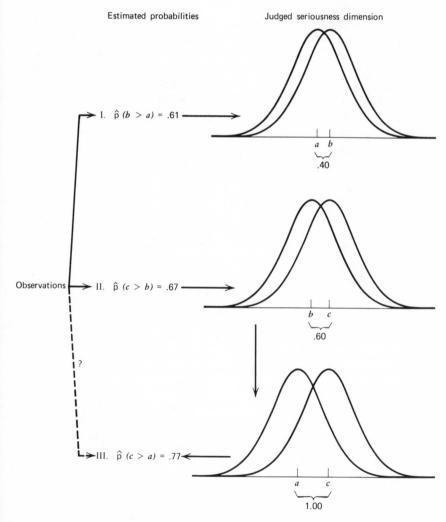

FIGURE 3.

relatively serious crime, although in many states (e.g., Michigan) it is a misdemeanor punishable by as little as a $15 fine.

But reasonable results alone are not enough to establish the validity of the measurement technique. Instead, this validity is evaluated by determining whether the technique is *consistent*—in the sense that the distances on the dimension may be used to predict confusions between crimes prior to the time this confusion is assessed empirically. Figure 3 illustrates how such consistency is evaluated.

Section I of Figure 3 illustrates a hypothetical situation in which the observations collected from a particular population lead an experimenter to estimate that the probability that crime b is judged to be more serious than crime a in that population is approximately .61. Applying the Thurstone measurement technique, the experimenter concludes that the difference between the mean of a's distribution and the mean of b's distribution on the seriousness dimension is .4 standard deviations,[2] as is illustrated on the right part of Section I. Section II illustrates a similar hypothetical comparison between crimes b and c; the experimenter estimates the probability that c is judged more serious than b to be approximately .67, which leads him to place c .6 standard deviations above b on the seriousness dimension. Given that the distance from a to b is .4 standard deviations and that from b to c is .6 standard deviations, the experimenter must now conclude that the distance between a and c is 1 standard deviation. This distance in turn leads to the conclusion that the probability that c should be judged more serious than a in the population is .77 if the model is consistent. If the experimenter's observations lead him to estimate this probability as equal or nearly equal to .77, the experimenter concludes that the measurement model is not inconsistent with his data. If the observations lead him to conclude that this probability is significantly different from .77, he must reject the measurement technique as being inconsistent with his observations. (The question of exactly what constitutes a "significant" difference will be discussed later.)

One important philosophical point must be made here. Observations can only lead to the conclusion that a measurement technique is consistent or that it must be rejected as inconsistent. Observations can never lead to the conclusion that the measurement technique is perfectly consistent—although as increasing numbers of observations fail to lead to rejection of the technique, confidence in its essential validity increases. Additional data *may* always later prove the technique to be inconsistent. Thus, a measurement technique has the same philosophical status as does a scientific theory in that data may always lead to the rejection of the theory, but may never prove it to be valid—that is, incapable of being

---

[2]It must be remembered that this method (Case 5) involves the assumption that all standard deviations are equal; hence, they are all equal to *the* stadard deviation, which may be regarded as a "unit of measurement."

rejected on the basis of future observations.[3] In fact, a measurement technique is a "miniature" theory (see Coombs, 1964).

Figure 4 illustrates how the same evaluation of consistency may be made of a much more common type of measurement—that of weight. As is illustrated in sections I and II of Figure 4, the assignment of a weight to an object is made on the basis of the number of standard weights (grams, ounces, pounds) it balances in a pan balance (see Adams, 1966). Once an assignment is made to more than one object, the weight assigned to objects placed together in a collection ("concatenated") is the sum of the individual weights. Any weight that perfectly balances this collection is assigned the same weight assigned to the collection, and this weight then determines how many standard weights the object should balance, as illustrated in sections III and IV of Figure 4.

Thus, seriousness and weight are both evaluated in terms of the consistency of the measurement techniques. There may well be situations in which judgments of seriousness of crimes lead to inconsistencies, in which case the Thurstone technique is rejected.

Thus, representational measurement involves the establishment of a two-way correspondence between: (1) some property of things being measured and (2) some property of the measurement scale. In the example of judged seriousness, the property of things being measured is the probability with which one is judged to be more serious than another; the property of the measurement scale is distance. In the example of weight, the property of the things being measured is their behavior in a pan balance; the property of the measurement scale is numerical extent (i.e., real number). The correspondence is two-way in that: (1) the property of the things being measured determines their value or position on the measurement scale and (2) these values or positions may in turn be used to make inferences about the property of the things being measured. Technically, when such a two-way correspondence exists, the measurement scale is said to *represent* the property of the things being measured. The things being measured considered together with the crucial property are said to form an *empirical relational system,* and the measurement scale considered together with its crucial property is said to form a *formal relational system;* the two-way correspondence is termed a *homeomorphism.* (For a more complete technical discussion of the nature of measurement scales, see Chapter 2 of Coombs, Dawes, and Tversky, 1970 and Suppes and Zinnes, 1963.)

Objects and events have many properties. As was carefully stated in the preceding paragraph, measurement involves a representation of *some* property— for example, judged seriousness, behavior in a pan balance. Hence, measuring

---

[3]This conclusion is an example of a very old principle, first espoused by the eighteenth century Scottish philosopher David Hume. No amount of experience can ever *prove* that our generalizations about reality are valid, since it is always possible that future experience will contradict these generalizations.

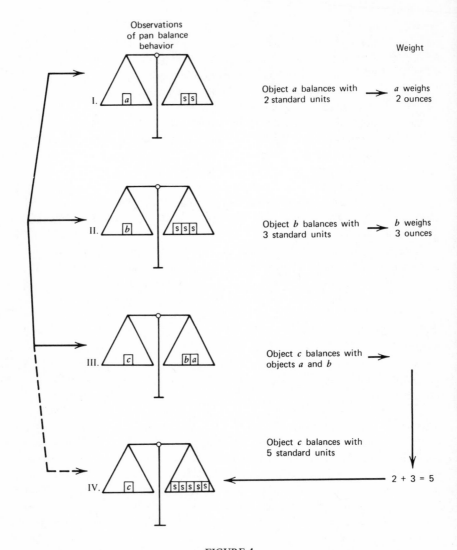

Observations
of pan balance
behavior

Weight

I. Object *a* balances with 2 standard units → *a* weighs 2 ounces

II. Object *b* balances with 3 standard units → *b* weighs 3 ounces

III. Object *c* balances with objects *a* and *b* →

IV. Object *c* balances with 5 standard units

2 + 3 = 5

FIGURE 4.

some property of an object does not involve its complete description. It follows that the complexity of the thing being measured is irrelevant to the question of whether some property may be measured successfully. Yet people will often maintain that attitudes (feelings, moods, etc.) cannot be measured because of their complexity—or because of their peculiar (i.e., human) characteristics. In an early article, Thurstone responded to this argument (1931, p. 19).

"One of the most frequent questions is that a score on an attitude scale, let us say of attitude toward God, does not truly describe the person's attitude. There are so many complex factors involved in a person's attitude on any social issue that it cannot be adequately described by a simple number such as a score on some sort of test or scale. This is quite true, but it is also equally true of all measurements.

"The measurement of any object or entity describes only one attribute [i.e., property] of the object measured. This is the universal characteristic of all measurement. When the height of a table is measured, the whole table has not been described but only that attribute which was measured."

2.2 Index Measurement

Consider an instructor who wishes to determine whether his students tend to approve or disapprove of smoking marijuana. He might just ask them. Then he finds out how many students say that they approve of smoking marijuana, how many say that they disapprove of smoking marijuana, and how many say that they neither approve nor disapprove. He then arrives at a conclusion such as: "Contrary to popular belief, x percentage of the students in my class say that they approve of smoking marijuana." Or he could try a slightly more elaborate technique; he could present each student with a *rating scale* of the type illustrated in Figure 5. Then, in addition to saying which proportion of his students approve, disapprove, or are indifferent, he might be able to say something about the distribution of approval and disapproval; for example, it might turn out that the students who approve tend to check the +3 category, perhaps indicating strong approval, whereas the students who disapprove check only the −1 category, perhaps indicating only mild disapproval. Furthermore, the instructor could compute the usual statistics that describe distributions of numbers—the mean, the variance, and so on.

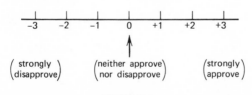

FIGURE 5.

Has the instructor really measured attitude toward marijuana? First, it should be pointed out that the instructor has realized that only properties are measured and, hence, he has attempted to evaluate only one aspect of attitude toward marijuana—approval or disapproval. But what do the students' responses to the

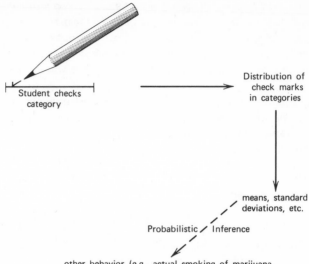

Student checks
category

Distribution of
check marks
in categories

means, standard
deviations, etc.

Probabilistic / Inference

other behavior (e.g., actual smoking of marijuana,
avoiding or approaching other people who smoke
marijuana, lobbying for or against its legalization.)

FIGURE 6.

rating scale really mean? Do these responses consitute the sort of behavior discussed in the previous section—that is, behavior that is systematic and may be systematically represented by a scale of measurement? The answer is no.

There is no representational measurement here because there is nothing in the numbers the instructor obtains that constrains the actual or potential checking behavior of the students. Hence, the numbers do not constitute a scale of measurement—in the sense that some property of the scale mirrors a crucial property of the thing being measured. The situation is illustrated in Figure 6, which should be contrasted with Figure 3 and 4.

Since the correspondence established is one-way instead of two-way, the resulting process will here be termed *index measurement.* That is, index measurement occurs whenever a property of the thing being indexed determines a corresponding index, but not *vice versa.* In the previous example, the checking behavior of the students determined the distribution of the numbers from −3 to +3, their mean, their standard deviation, and so on, but this distribution of numbers cannot be used to make inferences about checking behavior not yet observed. (Contrast this example with that of weight—where the numbers assigned to objects yield predictions about which will balance or outweigh which prior to the time that they are placed in a pan balance.)

Representational measurement was evaluated in terms of its internal consistency. How should index measurement be evaluated? The answer presented here is that it should be evaluated in terms of its usefulness. If, for example, the instructor can use his numbers to predict which groups of students will support politicians proposing an end to the prohibition on marijuana, which groups of students will tend to smoke marijuana themselves, or which groups of students will tend to avoid association with marijuana smokers, then these numbers have utility. If, however, no such results can be established, then these numbers have little utility.

Notice that both representational measurement and index measurement are evaluated in terms of predictability—the main difference being that representational measurement is evaluated in terms of how well it can predict a certain specific property of the thing being measured, whereas index measurement is evaluated in terms of a much more vague standard of general usefulness. For example, the Gross National Product (GNP) is a well-defined number that is a useful *index* of economic wealth. The GNP can be used to predict many events external to itself; for example, a rise in total income without a simultaneous rise in GNP may portend rising prices and possible international monetary problems (if such an inflationary condition is not present in other countries). Such predictions have two important qualities that differentiate them from the predictions made by representational measures; they are about events *external* to those used to obtain the index, and they are not certain. In contrast, predictions made on the basis of representational measurement, such as weight, are about the same class of events used to obtain the measures (e.g., pan balance behaviors), and they are certain (at least within a margin of "error"—resulting from, for example, minor malfunctioning of the balance used). Similarities between representational measurement and index measurement will be discussed in the final chapter of this book; for the present, it is important to understand their dissimilarity—specifically, the difference between the two-way correspondence established in representational measurement and the one-way correspondence established by index measurement.

Index measurement, involving only a one-way correspondence, occurs whenever there is a specifiable rule that leads to assignment of measurement scale values. The rule need not be consistent in the sense that the measurement scale values in turn imply certain properties of the objects being indexed. Since there are an indeterminately large number of rules that could be specified to assign numbers to properties of objects, there are an indeterminately large number of index measurement systems. It would be possible, for example, to index women by assigning values to them on the basis of their eye color, hair color, skin texture, bust size, waist size, and so on; moreover, the infinite variety of ways in which these numbers could be assigned determine an infinite number of index measurement systems. These values would be useful, however, only if they were related to something else of interest—for example, male ratings of overall physical attractiveness.

2.3 Attitude

As was pointed out at the beginning of Chapter I, attitudes are more easily measured than defined. In fact, in the article in which Allport made this observation (1935), he considers a variety of definitions; five are listed below.

1. *Attitude* connotes a neuropsychic state of readiness for mental and physical activity (p. 4).

2. *Attitudes* are individual mental processes which determine both the actual and potential responses of each person in a social world. Since an attitude is always directed toward some object it may be defined as "state of mind of the individual toward a value" (p. 6).

3. *Attitude*... preparation or readiness for response (p. 8).

4. *Attitude* is a mental and neural state of readiness organized through experience exerting a directive or dynamic influence upon the individual's response to all objects and situations with which it is related (p. 8).

5. *Attitude*... "degree of affect" for or against an object or a value (p. 10).

More recently another, commonly accepted, definition has been proposed by Katz (1960).

6. *Attitude* is the predisposition of the individual to evaluate some symbol or object or aspect of his world in a favorable or unfavorable manner. . . . Attitudes include the affective, or feeling core of liking or disliking, and the cognitive, or belief, elements which describe the effect of the attitude, its characteristics, and its relations to other objects (p. 168).

The above list should convince the reader that although "representational measurement" and "index measurement" have an exact scientific meaning (hence definition), "attitude" does not. When social psychologists speak of attitude, they are *generally* speaking about an affect or a preparedness to respond in a certain way toward a social object or phenomenon. Moreover, they would generally agree that attitude involves some evaluative component—that is, affect is for or against, preparedness is to accept or to reject. It follows, then, that techniques meant to measure attitudes generally require an individual to respond in a positive or negative manner to a social object (Guttman, 1970).

But there is really no necessity that social psychologists agree about the definition of attitude in order to measure attitudes. All that can be measured are specific properties. If, then, one person wishes to argue that something that has been measured is a property of an attitude, and another person wishes to argue that it is not, they may do so without in any way affecting the measurement process—or the validity of the resulting measurement scale.

This book presents examples generally regarded as involving attitudes; the examples will involve the response of an individual to a social object or phenomenon, and the response will have affective or evaluative connotations.

QUESTIONS

1. Is measurement of sensation in terms of just noticeable differences (jnd's) representational measurement in the sense defined in this chapter? *(Hint:*

what crucial property of two objects is implied by the fact that one is 2 jnd's more intense than another?)

2. What happens to confusion methods if objects are perfectly discriminable? Should all lights that are perceived 100 percent of the time to be brighter than other lights be placed at the same distance above the other lights on the brightness scale? Would such placement be possible?

3. How would the social psychologist attempting to measure judged seriousness of crimes using Thurstone's technique deal with the problem that all his subjects say that murder is more serious than vagrancy, and all say that murder is more serious than robbery?

4. Consider the following definition of measurement (Stevens, 1951, p. 1; 1968, p. 854): "the assignment of numbers to objects or events according to rules." How many different ways could we measure feminine beauty according to this definition?

5. The psychologist Thorndike wrote in 1913 "whatever exists, exists in some quantity; whatever exists in quantity can be measured." Discuss this statement in light of the definitions of representational and index measurement presented in this chapter.

6. Discuss the argument that things must be measured if they are to be studied scientifically and that, therefore, attitudes must be measured before they can be studied. Discuss the counterargument that attitudes are too complex to be measured.

7. Index measures are evaluated in terms of their usefulness. Should not representational measures be also? In what sense are representational measures always useful?

Representational Measurement

Four classes of representational measurement techniques are presented in Chapters III to VI: *magnitude* techniques, *proximity* techniques, *interlocking* techniques, and *unfolding* techniques. Chapter VII deals with some general issues concerning representational techniques. In particular, Coombs' (1964) framework for classifying representational measurement is presented in this chapter, and it is demonstrated that all representational techniques belong to one of the four classes discussed in the preceding chapters; in addition, the concepts of "scale type," "fundamental measurement," and "functional measurement". are introduced and discussed.

III

Magnitude Techniques

3.1 Introduction

Thurstone's technique of comparative judgment is a magnitude technique. The judged seriousness of crimes is represented by the location of these crimes on a measurement scale; the order of these crimes on the scale, and the degree to which one crime is ordered above another, reflect the judgments of comparative seriousness.

When applying this technique, the investigator must have determined which crucial property he is interested in measuring (e.g., judged seriousness), and he must collect data from a subject (or subjects) that he can represent by order, or directional difference, on his measurement scale. The decision about which crucial property to investigate is common to all magnitude techniques, and the resulting measurement scale is meant to represent the order and magnitude of stimuli (or people) with respect to that property. As will be pointed out in Chapter IV, there are measurement techniques that do not involve the specification of a particular property prior to collecting data.

Since Thurstone's method of comparative judgment has been discussed at some length in Chapter II, other magnitude techniques will be presented in this chapter: specifically, the techniques involving *direct estimation* and the technique of *bisection*. (See Stevens, 1966, for a discussion of both techniques; he is presently the chief advocate of direct estimation techniques, especially in the field of attitude measurement.)

3.2 Direct Estimation Techniques

All direct estimation techniques involve the following sequence of steps: the investigator decides which property of a particular set of stimuli he is interested in studying; he specifies this property to his subjects, and then he presents them with the stimuli; on the basis of this property, subjects assign numbers to the stimuli, or to the differences between stimuli, or to the ratio of stimuli (or even to the ratio of differences between stimuli). The location of the stimuli on the measurement scale is determined directly from these numbers; that is, numbers

20

are assigned to the stimuli in such a way that the (relative) distances between or ratios of these numbers correspond to the subjects' judgments about these differences or ratios.

When the subjects "assign numbers on the basis of the property," they are to do so on the basis of their subjective impression about the degree to which the property is present in the stimuli, or about the location of the stimuli on the dimension defined by the property. For example, brightness is a property generally considered to be one of degree, whereas pitch is a property generally regarded as being one defined by location (see Stevens, 1951). In the domain of attitude measurement, it is not always clear whether a property is one of degree or location; which, for example, is "liberalism"?

Were the subjects to assign numbers haphazardly, there would be no measurement involved; instead, there would be at best index measurement (depending on whether the investigator specifies a rule to convert the numbers to scale values). Once, however, certain numerical judgments are made, then others are implied if the judge is to be consistent, that is, if there is to be true representational measurement. Two types of consistency—that involving intervals and that involving ratios—are most often evaluated.

Interval Consistency

The sum of the intervals between a and b and b and c must equal the interval between a and c. If, for example, a subject says politician a is 10 units more liberal than politician b, and politician b is 10 units more liberal than politician

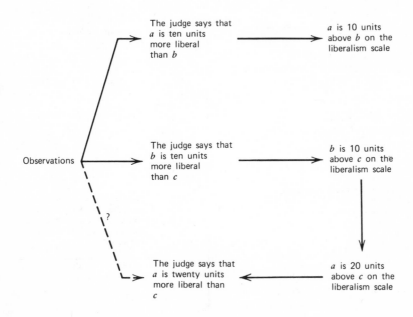

FIGURE 1.

c, he must then say that politician *a* is 20 units more liberal than politician *c*. This conclusion follows from the fact that 10 + 10 = 20 in the real number system, and this fact then constrains the behavior of the people assigning numbers if their behavior is to be represented by this system. See Figure 1; the implication here is based on the fact that $(a - b) + (b - c) = (a - c)$.

Ratio Consistency

The product of the ratio of *a* to *b* and *b* to *c* must equal the ratio of *a* to *c*. If,

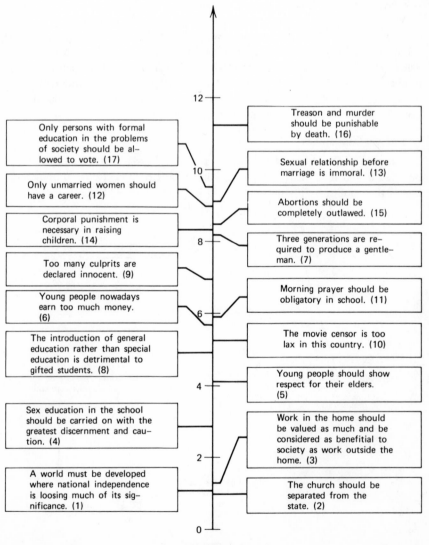

FIGURE 2.

for example, politician a is judged to be twice as liberal as politician b, and politician b is judged to be twice as liberal as politician c, then politician a must be judged to be four times as liberal as politician c. The implication here is based on the fact that $(a/b) \times (b/c) = (a/c)$; it is similar to that illustrated in Figure 1.

In effect, what is being done is to use people's subjective impressions and their knowledge of the number scale as a pan balance. The hope is that just as numbers are assigned to objects in consistent ways by the pan balance, people will assign numbers in consistent ways. Generally, when the consistency criterion is one of interval consistency, then people are asked to make interval judgments: for example, what is the difference in liberalism between politician a and b? When the consistency criterion is one of ratios, people are generally asked to make ratio judgments: for example, what is the ratio of politician b's liberalism to politician a's?

Ekman and Künnapas (1963) obtained judgments concerning 17 statements expressing conservative attitudes; 82 Swedish psychology students made ratio estimates of the degree of conservatism expressed by these statements. The resulting conservatism scale is presented in Figure 2, where the statements are represented "in their proper position" (p. 330). (The authors probably looked at the mean ratio estimates to determine these "proper positions.")

Figure 3 presents judgments concerning preference for 17 different occupations collected from 74 students at the University of Stockholm (Künnapas & Wikström, 1963). Both ratio judgments and interval judgments were used in collecting this data. The resulting scales, which were constructed by representing each occupation by the median number assigned it, turned out to be identical except for the zero point and the unit of measurement; hence, Figure 3 illustrates both these scales.

The question arises of how consistent interval or ratio estimates must be in order to serve as a basis for measurement. There is no answer that would currently be accepted by everyone using these estimates. At the one extreme, Stevens and his followers tend to regard any inconsistency as random error and accept the idea that people can make such estimates meaningfully—even if they conflict with one another. The human being is treated, in effect, like a scale with a worn spring; occasional inconsistencies are to be expected; they are from imperfections in the measuring instrument instead of from any basic problem in the conceptualization. At the other extreme, investigators design experiments specifically to challenge some of the implications of the direct estimate measurement techniques; if these implications are successfully challenged, the investigator concludes that the measurement technique is invalid—at least in the context he has studied. The issue of consistency will be discussed again in Section 3.4.

3.3 Bisection Methods

The direct estimation methods involve both subjects' reactions to stimuli and their use of numerical ratings. Several psychologists have raised the question of

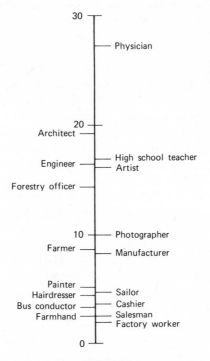

FIGURE 3.

whether people can really meaningfully make such numerical ratings. These psychologists have suggested that it might be more psychologically meaningful to ask subjects to manipulate stimuli themselves instead of to attempt to assign numbers to them (see Fagot & Stewart, 1970). Specifically, instead of presenting two stimuli and asking for some ratio or interval estimation these psychologists have presented subjects with two stimuli and asked them to produce or select a stimulus halfway between them with respect to the property being evaluated— that is, that *bisects* them.[1] The locations of the stimuli on the measurement scale are determined by assigning numbers to the stimuli in such a way that the number assigned to a stimulus bisecting two others is halfway between the numbers assigned to these two.

There are many ways to evaluate the consistency of bisection methods (see Pfanzagl, 1968). The most common consistency requirement is named, quite appropriately, the *bisection* condition. Suppose stimulus *c* is chosen as bisecting

[1]The judgment is simple psychologically because all the subject must do is to compare the two intervals between the stimulus he selects and the two with which he was presented; if the two intervals are unequal subjectively, he has not chosen the stimulus exactly halfway between the two presented; conversely, when he has selected a stimulus that bisects them, the intervals between them and the stimulus he selects are equal.

stimuli *a* and *e;* suppose further that stimulus *b* is chosen as bisecting stimuli *a* and *c*, and stimulus *d* is chosen as bisecting stimuli *c* and *e*; then, stimulus *c* must be chosen as bisecting stimuli *b* and *d*, as illustrated in Figure 4. The necessity of

FIGURE 4.

this condition can be seen by assigning numbers 1 to stimulus *a* and 5 to stimulus *e*; then *c*, since it bisects *a* and *e*, must be assigned the number 3; it follows that stimulus *b*, since it bisects *a* and *c*, must be assigned the number 2; similarly, stimulus *d* must be assigned the number 4, and since 3 is halfway between 2 and 4, it follows that stimulus *c* must bisect stimuli *b* and *d*.

One special type of bisection deserves mention. It is the type in which people are asked to produce or select stimuli that are either half or twice as intense as other stimuli; in effect, the subject is asked to bisect a pair of stimuli where one of the stimuli is a subjective zero point. Again, the bisection condition must be satisfied if bisection is to be consistent.

The most commonly used magnitude techniques in attitude scaling are direct estimation techniques and confusion techniques. The bisection technique, despite its greater simplicity than estimation methods, has not yet been used to much advantage in attitude measurement, perhaps because it is more difficult to construct or select social stimuli than physical stimuli. Nevertheless, there is no inherent reason why the bisection technique could not be used to measure attitudes.

3.4 Magnitude Techniques as Index Measures

Often, investigators are concerned not with the internal consistency of magnitude techniques, but instead with their use in generating numbers to predict external criteria. Although—as was discussed in Section 3.2—it is possible to *assume* that the techniques are internally consistent, it is also possible to be unconcerned with the consistency problem. For example, paired comparisons, interval estimates, or ratio estimates may be used to assign numerical values to the degree of liberalism of attitude statements, and then the numbers assigned to the statements endorsed by various people may be used to predict whether these people will vote on the liberal or conservative side of a particular issue. Both this assignment and subsequent prediction may be made in the absence of any attempt to evaluate the consistency of the paired comparisons, interval estimates, or ratio estimates. If the numbers predict, they predict. In such a context of unconcern, the numbers are used as indices, not representational measures.

Two points must be made about the use of magnitude techniques to generate indices. First, it is incumbent on the investigator who uses the techniques in this manner to *demonstrate* that the numbers obtained do, in fact, predict some criterion of interest (just as it is incumbent on the investigator who claims to have representational measures to demonstrate that these measures are consistent). The assignment of numbers in the absence of any empirical demonstration of validity is not "measurement" in any sense. Second, the question of whether the numbers obtained are representational measures or indices is not answered by determining the way in which they were generated—that is, it is not answered by investigating the nature of the observations per se. Instead, it is answered by the *assumptions* made about these observations and the *use* to which they are put. (Note: Not all psychologists would agree with this statement.) If the investigator assumes that all inconsistency is random error, then he may claim his numbers to be representational measures; of course, other investigators may challenge his claim by arguing that the inconsistency is too great or that it is systematic. If the investigator believes that his numbers are simply useful predictors, he may regard them as indices; here, there is the unlikely possibility that other investigators will argue that the numbers are so consistent that they must be regarded as true representational measures.

The distinction between observation per se and the nature of the observations will be discussed further in Section 7.2.

QUESTIONS

1. Consider measurement based on subjects' judgments that certain stimuli are half or twice as intense as other stimuli on the psychological dimension of interest. Restate the bisection condition for such a measurement.
2. In the text of this chapter, numerical examples were used to demonstrate the bisection condition. Show algebraically why this condition must be satisfied.
3. When conservatism was assessed by Ekman and Künnapas, they considered only conservative statements. Suppose, however, they had included both liberal and conservative statements in their pool. Could they then have used a ratio-estimation technique? (What sense would it make to ask a subject to judge the ratio of conservatism in a conservative statement to that in a liberal statement?)
4. In general, a distinction may be made between what could be called a *bipolar* attribute and a *unipolar* attribute. A bipolar attribute is one defined by having two different ends (e.g., left versus right); a unipolar attribute extends from some zero point. Discuss the problems of direct estimation for bipolar attributes.
5. Let the stimulus that bisects stimuli a and b be symbolized $a \cdot b$. The bisection condition may then be expressed as:

$$(a \cdot e) = (a \cdot (a \cdot e)) \cdot ((a \cdot e) \cdot e)$$

Explain in words. Now consider a further condition:

bisymmetry: $(a \cdot b) \cdot (c \cdot d) = (a \cdot c) \cdot (b \cdot d)$

Demonstrate that this condition must be satisfied if bisection judgments are consistent.

6. If Thurstone had used ratio or interval estimates to measure the seriousness of crimes, is there any reason why he should obtain the same measurement scale that he obtained using his technique of comparative judgments?

7. Suppose one investigator uses a confusion technique to measure the degree of conservatism in a set of statements, whereas another investigator uses an interval estimation technique. Suppose further that the two investigators obtain different measurement scales. A critic argues that since the investigators have conflicting results, neither scale represents *the true degree of conservatism* in the statements. Critically evaluate his argument.

IV

Proximity Techniques

4.1 Introduction

Consider the emotional attitudes conveyed by statements expressing love, or grief, or contempt. Such statements could be evaluated—by the magnitude methods discussed in Chapter III—in terms of pleasantness of the emotion; that is, paired comparison judgments, interval estimates, or ratio estimates could be used to locate the statements on a dimension of pleasantness. Or the statements could be evaluated in terms of the degree to which they express love versus hate; that is, one of the magnitude techniques could be used to locate the statements on a dimension of lovingness.

But which dimension is more important in the perception of emotional attitude: pleasantness or lovingness? Magnitude techniques cannot be used to answer this question because they require the investigator to specify in advance the dimension (property) of the attitude that he wishes to measure. The resulting magnitude scale will be important only to the degree to which it is an important property to the subject(s) being investigated. Often, in the domain of attitude measurement, *no* justification is made for the assumption of importance, and the only reason for believing that this assumption is correct is that the investigator himself lives in the same society as do those people he is investigating—and, hence, has some valid idea about which properties of attitudes are important in that society.

This problem with magnitude scaling was first emphasized by the philosopher Nelson Goodman in his book *The Structure of Appearance* (1951). Although he was concerned with more classical problems in psychophysical judgment, his basic argument is equally applicable to attitude measurement. It is that magnitude techniques beg the basic question of perception: What *are* the basic dimensions, or properties, that best describe our perception of reality? When an individual is asked to judge the brightness of lights, it is assumed—not demonstrated—that brightness is an important dimension of his visual perception. Similarly, when an individual is asked to judge how liberal or conservative a statement of opinion is, it is assumed—not demonstrated—that the liberal-conservative dimension is important in his perception of opinion statements.

Goodman suggested that in several contexts these assumptions may be premature, and that it would be better to ask the subject to behave in ways in which the investigator could *discover* the important dimensions.

Goodman further proposed (1951, Section 2, Chapter IX) that in place of asking subjects for magnitude judgments, investigators should ask subjects for matching judgments; that is, instead of asking for some behavior that allows the placement of stimuli on a dimension determined a priori, the investigator asks which stimuli match other stimuli and then attempts to *infer* what dimension or dimensions underlie such matching judgments. If, for example, the liberal-conservative dimension were important for a particular individual's perception of opinion statements, then statements that were alike on this dimension would be said to match, and statements that were unlike on this dimension would be said not to match; or, in other words, if the investigator were to build a spatial representation of the opinion statements by representing those that match as near each other, he would find that an important dimension in his representation is that of liberalism-conservatism.

With the exception of Galanter (1956), few investigators have used judgments of matching in the manner suggested by Goodman. Instead, they have usually used judgments of similarity or dissimilarity, or the degree to which stimuli are confused. The basic measurement technique has been to represent the stimuli by points in a space in such a way that the judgments of dissimilarity or the confusability of these stimuli is represented by the distance between the points; in general, the more dissimilar or less confused the stimuli, the farther apart they are represented in the space.

For example, Dawes and Kramer (1966) investigated the confusability of attitudes conveyed by vocally expressed emotion. Their work is relevant to the question raised earlier in this chapter: Is pleasantness or lovingness a more important dimension in the perception of attitudes conveyed by such expressions? Dawes and Kramer describe their procedure for obtaining confusions as follows (1966, p. 572):

"Five short scripts were prepared, each designed to portray a different emotion: anger, contempt, indifference, grief, *and* love. *Each script contained a common set of words modified from a test passage used by Fairbanks (1940), Fairbanks and Hoaglin (1941), and Fairbanks and Pronovost (1939). Six experienced student actors made recordings of the scripts. From these recordings, a separate tape recording was made containing only the common test passage:*

'There is no other answer. You've asked me that before. My reply has always been the same, and it will always be the same.'

"There were five readings each from attempts to portray anger, grief, and indifference; three readings of contempt, and four of love. These were arranged on the tape in random order.

"In addition, the 22 passages were copied onto another tape through a low-pass filter. All frequencies above 400 cps were severely attenuated. This type

Table 1   Proportions of Confusion: Ordinary Recordings

	Anger	Contempt	Indifference	Grief	Love
Anger	75	25	0	0	0
Contempt	5	85	10	5	0
Indifference	0	15	75	5	5
Grief	0	5	5	60	30
Love	0	*15*	*10*	15	55

Table 2   Proportions of Confusion: Filtered Recordings

	Anger	Contempt	Indifference	Grief	Love
Anger	75	25	0	0	0
Contempt	5	50	35	5	5
Indifference	5	10	65	*5*	*15*
Grief	0	5	5	70	20
Love	0	10	20	20	50

of attenuation has been used in several studies to make verbal content unrecognizable, while preserving some of the nonverbal properties of the speech pattern (Kramer, 1963). A different random order was used for the filtered passages.

"Twenty-seven male Ss heard first the filtered and then the unfiltered passages over high fidelity earphones. Ss were asked to match each reading with the one emotion that best fitted it. They had to choose from among the five emotions that the original scripts had been designed to portray. Ss were not told that the filtered and unfiltered passages were the same. Because only the common test passage was heard, the particular words could be of no help in distinguishing among the five emotions; the actors' voices provided the only available cues."

The results from the ordinary recordings are presented in Table 1, those for the filtered recordings in Table 2. The entries in these tables refer to the proportion of times the subjects identified the row emotion as the column emotion; these proportions are rounded to the nearest 5 percent.

As observed by the authors (1966, p. 573):

". . . the entries in each row increase until the diagonal and then decrease. Thus, if these probabilities are interpreted as measures of psychological similarity, proximity analysis yields a single dimension 'running' from anger to love. Moreover, the dimension has the following distance relations."

The dimension is clearly one of *lovingness* (note the proximity of love and grief). A spatial representation of this dimension is presented in Figure 1; with the exception of the italicized confusions, the distances on this dimension represent the proportions of confusion—the closer the emotions on the dimension, the more confused they are.

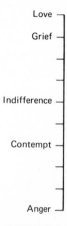

FIGURE 1.

Confusions and judgements of dissimilarities or similarities are indicators of *psychological proximity*. The exact way in which such predicators of psychological proximity are represented in the space is determined by the exact *proximity technique* employed. For example, some techniques involve numerical rating of similarity or dissimilarity and then produce a space in which these numerical ratings are represented precisely by the numerical distances between the points representing the objects being rated. (These ratings may either be taken from a single subject, or they may be averaged ratings from a pool of subjects.) At the other extreme, certain techniques involve only ratings of which stimuli are more or less similar to which others, and the representation constructed reflects only the order of the similarity ratings. For example, a subject may be asked to judge whether a particular object *a* is more like object *b* or object *c,* and the space constructed requires only that object *a* is represented as closer to object *b* or object *c,* depending on his judgment. (Again, the similarity judgments for each subject may be analyzed separately, or they may be pooled in some way.) Techniques that require the similarity or dissimilarity judgments to be represented by the numerical distance between points representing the objects are generally termed *metric* techniques, whereas those requiring the judgments to be represented only by the order of distances between the points representing the objects are commonly termed *nonmetric* techniques. The former techniques have been developed chiefly by Abelson (1954), Torgerson (1958), and Tucker and Messick (1963), and the latter techniques have been developed primarily by Coombs (1964), Guttman and Lingoes (see Lingoes, 1965, 1966, 1968), Kruskal (1964a, 1964b), and Shepard (1962a, 1962b). All these techniques are termed *proximity* techniques because what is represented is the psychological proximity or nearness of various objects (such as attitudes). The technique represents the psychological proximity by spatial proximity.

4.2 Another Example

An example of a nonmetric proximity technique may be found in Coombs (1964, pp. 455-456). Coombs analyzed some data collected by Rokeach (1960, pp. 295-296), which involved judged similarities of different religions. Rokeach had asked subjects of different religions to judge how similar other religions were to theirs; the actual procedure is described as follows.

"Subjects are presented with a mimeographed list of religions in alphabetical order, as follows:

> *Atheist*
> *Baptist*
> *Catholic*
> *Episcopalian*
> *Jewish*
> *Lutheran*
> *Methodist*
> *Mohammedan*
> *Presbyterian*

"A number of blank lines follow this list. The subject is simply asked to write the name of his own religion on the first line, the name of the religion most similar to his own on the second line, and so on. The least similar religion is written on the last line. *

"We do not define what we mean by 'similarity.' Each subject decides this for himself.

"The mean similarity rank assigned to each of the nine religions was determined separately for six groups of college students: Catholics, Episcopalians, Presbyterians, Lutherans, Methodists, and Baptists. The reason these six groups of subjects were used and no other is simply that they are the denominations most frequently found in our samples. Other Christian denominations, Jews, etc., were found too infrequently to warrant separate study.

"Table 3 may be read as follows: The Catholics, on the average, judged the Episcopalians to be most similar to themselves, followed by the Lutheran, Presbyterian, Methodist, and Baptist denominations. Then follow the Jews, Mohammedans, and Atheists."

Since no Jews, Mohammedans, or Atheists were included in the data collection, and since these three religions were seen as least similar to all the other religions, they were excluded from Coombs' analysis. Using a technique of Frank Goode's, Coombs constructed a single dimension on which the other six religions were represented. See Figure 2.

---

*A tenth group, ex-Catholic, was also on the list. But this turned out to mean so many different things to different subjects that we dropped it from further study.

Table 3   The Similarity Matrix

Rank Order of Similarity

Group	Number	1	2	3	4	5	6	7	8
Catholic	120	Epis.	Luth.	Pres.	Meth.	Bapt.	Jew	Moham.	Ath.
Episcopalian	38	Cath.	Luth.	Pres.	Meth.	Bapt.	Jew	Moham.	Ath.
Lutheran	57	Pres.	Meth.	Epis.	Bapt.	Cath.	Jew	Moham.	Ath.
Presbyterian	100	Meth.	Bapt.	Luth.	Epis.	Cath.	Jew	Moham.	Ath.
Methodist	116	Pres.	Bapt.	Luth.	Epis.	Cath.	Jew	Moham.	Ath.
Baptist	26	Meth.	Pres.	Luth.	Epis.	Cath.	Jew	Moham.	Ath.

FIGURE 2.

This dimension was constructed so that the rank order of the distances from each religion to every other religion corresponded to the rank order of the judged similarities of the other religions to it; for example, Lutheranism is 4.5 units distance from Presbyterianism, 5.6 units distance from Methodism, 6.8 units distance from Episcopalianism, 8.1 units distance from Baptist, and 9.1 distance from Catholicism; inspection of Table 3 confirms that the rank order of these distances correponds to the rank order of judged similarity of the other five religions to Lutheranism. The dimension constructed by Coombs and Goode is perfect in that every such rank order is perfectly represented.

Now, having constructed spatial representation of the similarity judgments and having discovered that these judgments may be represented on a single dimension, Coombs asked what the dimension might mean. (Remember Goodman's suggestion was that one purpose of letting dimensions and properties be defined by the subjects' behavior instead of a priori by the investigator is that the investigator may *discover* relevant dimensions.) Coombs has no simple answer, nor is one proposed here. To quote Coombs (1964, p. 456):

"Just what interpretation this continuum might best be given is not absolutely clear, but a possibility is that it represents a scale of degree of prescribed ritual, diminishing from left to right, as perceived by these college students.

"The question naturally arises as to just what value such a scale has—is it related to other behavior or just judgments of similarity? Rokeach examined church records in Lansing, Michigan, from two churches in each of five denominations. He found that the relative migration of new members to a

church from others and the relative migration from a church to other denominations are functions of their similarity as measured on the similarity scale. He also studied interfaith marriages and found that the frequency of interfaith marriage varies directly with judged interfaith similarity. These results support the contention that similarity analysis may be used to reveal the cognitive and perceptual structure of individuals in significant areas of behavior."

The observations on which this example is based were verbal judgments of similarity, which were then averaged. As was mentioned earlier, such judgments are not the only types of behavior that can be analyzed by proximity techniques. There are, in fact, a large range of behaviors that may be interpreted as indicating psychological proximity; confusion, which was discussed in the earlier part of this chapter, is one among many others. For example, subjects may be presented with attitude statements and asked to sort them into piles according to any criteria, schemes, or intuitions they have about the statements; then the proportion of times two statements are put in the same pile can be used as a measure of the psychological proximity of the two statements for the subjects doing the sorting. Rinn (1963) has, in fact, used this technique to assess graduate students' attitudes toward various classroom behaviors. To quote from the abstract of his paper (1963, p. 173):

". . . Twenty-seven graduate students gave free response descriptions of their own classroom behavior. Each student then divided the set of statements into two or more categories on an idiosyncratic basis. Frequency of joint inclusion in a distinct category was used as a measure of the similarity of pairs of stimuli. Coombs' [nonmetric proximity] procedure yielded two dimensions of simple orders of stimulus statements which were interpreted as involvement and feeling tone. Investigation of other phenomenological issues by the methodology was recommended."

One distinction between Rokeach's study and Rinn's study should be noted. In Rokeach's study, subjects were asked to assess the relative similarity of each religion *to* a specified religion; in Rinn's study, in contrast, the psychological proximity of each pair of statements was assessed in a symmetric way. Noting how often statements *a* and *b* were put in the same categories did not lead to an estimate of how psychologically proximal statement *a* was to statement *b* separate from an estimate of how psychologically proximal statement *b* was to statement *a*; instead, it estimated *the* psychological proximity of the two statements. The type of observation made in the Rokeach study has been termed by Coombs an indicator of *conditional* proximity, whereas that obtained in Rinn's study has been termed *symmetric* indicator of proximity (see Coombs, 1963). The distinction between these two types of measures will become important in Section 4.3, where tests of the consistency of proximity techniques are discussed. Of course, the *representation* of the psychological proximity is always symmetric because distance is symmetric.

Finally, it should be noted that in both studies the proximity measures used were based on group data. There is no necessity that proximity measures be based on group data and, in fact, one of the strengths of proximity techniques is that it is possible to assess psychological proximity for single individuals; thus, it is possible to compare individuals, for example, in terms of the configuration of points representing their judgments, in terms of the dimensionality of their spaces, and so on.

4.3 Consistency Checks

As has been emphasized in this chapter and in Chapter II, the consistency of a measurement technique is evaluated by working out implications of the numerical representation and then checking to see whether these implications are satisfied in the data. The examples given in both these chapters were of numerical scales representing a single property, and the implications were always based on distances along these scales. Furthermore, these implications were quite precise in that numerical values could be obtained from the distances—values that in turn placed exact constraints on the behavior of the objects being measured. (Again refer back to Figures 2 and 3 of Chapter II.)

In contrast, the consistency criteria used for evaluating proximity techniques are less precise, and less well understood. In fact, prior to the work of Beals, Krantz, and Tversky (1968), there have been virtually no attempts to assess the consistency of nonmetric proximity techniques—although the consistency of metric proximity techniques was either taken for granted or rejected on the basis of some glaring inconsistency in the data.

The problem with evaluating the consistency of proximity techniques is that the constraints certain distances impose on others are not exact constraints, and hence the implications about observations are inexact. The problem is further exacerbated in the case of nonmetric techniques because these techniques, in addition, do not involve an exact relationship between proximity measures and their representation by a distance in the space; only the order of the proximity measures must be represented by the order of the distances.

The fact that certain distances do not place exact constraints on others is illustrated by the following example. Suppose the distance between points a and b is three units and that between points b and c is two units; if the three points lie on a single line, then the distance between points a and c must either be one unit or five units (depending on the order of the points on the line); if, however, the points do not lie on a single line—and there is nothing in the proximity techniques that demand that they do—then the only constraint placed upon the distance between a and c is that it be less than five units and more than one, because no side of a triangle may be longer than the sum of the other two sides.

But any distance less than five and more than one unit is possible. And in general, the constraints distances place on each other in a multidimensional space are of this form. The requirement that no side of a triangle may be longer than the sum of the other two sides, a requirement often termed the *triangle inequality*, implies that certain distances may not be greater or less than certain values, but it does not yield any more exact information.

Thus, the triangle inequality places constraints on distances, but constraints of a much less exact nature than those found in Chapter III. A more exact constraint is placed by the conditions that distance be symmetric; that is, that the distance between *a* and *b* be equal to the distance between *b* and *a*. But this constraint is applicable only when conditional indicators of psychological proximity are to be represented. For when symmetric indicators are to be represented, there is no distinction in the observations between the proximity of *a* to *b* and the proximity of *b* to *a*, and hence there can be no contradiction in the implications about the distance between *a* and *b* as opposed to the distance between *b* and *a*. When conditional proximity indicators are collected, however, this requirement of symmetry does impose constraints—as will be illustrated shortly.

Notice that the symmetry condition does *not* imply that the distances must be *relatively* symmetric, although they must—of course—be symmetric in an absolute sense; that is, the fact that *a* is the closest point to *b* does not imply that *b* must be the closest point to *a*, but only that the absolute distance between *a* and *b* be the same whichever way it is evaluated. Consider, for example, Figure 3; in that figure, *b* is the closest point to *a*, but *c* is closer to *b* than is *a*.

When metric techniques are employed, the triangle inequality can be violated, and when the techniques are applied to conditional proximity measures, the symmetry condition as well may be violated. The possibility of violation arises because metric proximity techniques associate a specific distance with each indicator of psychological proximity, and hence it is possible that the triangle inequality may be violated. When conditional proximity indicators are being represented by a metric technique, the symmetry condition as well may be violated. The fact that such violations *can* occur provides a way of evaluating the consistency of such techniques; when violations do not occur—or when they are minor—then the technique yields a true representation of the indicators of psychological proximity.

•
b

•   •
a   *c*

FIGURE 3.

Consider now nonmetric proximity techniques applied to symmetric proximity measures. These techniques can result in violations of *neither* the symmetry condition *nor* the triangle inequality. First, the symmetry condition cannot be violated because the psychological proximity of *a* to *b* is not evaluated separately from that of *b* to *a*. Second, the triangle inequality cannot be violated because, irrespective of the order of the indicators of psychological proximity, it is always possible to represent *n* objects in a space of *n* - 2 dimensions in such a way that the rank order of the distances represents the rank order of these indicators (as pointed out by Bennett, 1956).

Beals, Krantz, and Tversky (1968) have examined conditions other than the triangle inequality and the symmetry condition. These authors show first that if six specific conditions hold (p. 133), then it is possible to represent proximity measures by distance, and finally they show that one of these conditions (p. 140) is a *necessary* condition for proximity to be represented as distance. Although these authors make important points, they are not directly applicable as yet to the domain of attitude measurement, since the authors are considering the situation in which it is possible to construct stimuli corresponding to any specified points in the space. But in the domain of attitude measurement, there are often only a finite number of stimuli being considered, and hence it is not possible to construct stimuli corresponding to any specified point. Nevertheless, the approach of these authors may be extended to the finite case, and their basic criticism of proximity techniques—that methods currently in use "give a 'best' answer regardless of whether the underlying model is appropriate" (p. 127)—is important. Much the same point had been previously made by Torgerson (1965, p. 381), who wrote:

"The new procedures [nonmetric proximity techniques] would . . . seem to offer advantages over the old; to require very little and to yield very much. Yet there are many problems connected with these which . . . have not been at all obvious. . . . It's like doing a factor analysis. And, like factor analysis, the methods always yield an answer. But it can be even more difficult to fully comprehend the meaning of that answer."

Another method for evaluating nonmetric proximity techniques has recently been proposed by Klahr (1969). To understand Klahr's suggestion, it is first necessary to have more detailed knowledge than has yet been presented in this chapter of the mechanics of nonmetric proximity techniques. Although all these techniques have a common purpose—to represent the proximity measures by distance in such a way that the rank order of the distances corresponds to the rank order of the proximity measures—they differ in details. Some involve simple paper and pencil procedures (e.g., Coombs, 1964), some rely heavily on intuition, but most consist of a computer program for accomplishing the representation by "jiggling" (Gleason, 1967) an initially reasonable configuration of points until the measurement criterion is satisfied in the smallest number of dimensions. These programs *generally* give a good fit, in the sense that the rank order of distances corresponds almost perfectly to the rank order of proximity measures—and will give a good fit irrespective of the order of the proximity measures. The problem is that, as noted above, it is always possible to improve fit by simply increasing the number of dimensions of the space.

These techniques also present indices that are supposed to indicate how bad the fit is. (These indices are usually termed something like "stress.") Klahr has proposed that random numbers be used to simulate completely unstructured proximity indicators, and that the indicator of badness of fit for the random numbers in a particular number of dimensions be compared with this indicator based on the actual indicators of psychological proximity when represented in the same number of dimensions. Only if the measure is much smaller for the actual measures than for the randomly generated ones should the measurement technique be regarded as a good representation.

One possible drawback of the Klahr procedure is that certain proximity indicators may clearly violate the intent of proximity techniques without yielding as bad a fit as do randomly generated numbers. For example, it has been suggested (Messick, 1956) that an individual's perception of attitude statements may be assessed by asking him whether he thinks a person who endorses one statement would also endorse another. On the basis of the individual's judgments, the statements are to be represented in a space—which is to characterize his perception of other people's attitudes (p. 57):

"If a person who strongly agrees with one statement would not be very likely to agree with the other then the two statements can be considered to be psychologically far apart. If the psychological distance among attitude statements can be analyzed into a Cartesian space, it will be possible to obtain a configuration of the way in which an individual perceives attitudes as being structured in a given domain."

As Messick understood, there are problems with such an indicator of psychological proximity. First, the judgments may contain inherent asymmetries (and hence the spatial representation of the judgment may also); second, representations of the judgments may involve violations of the triangle inequality. To see these problems, consider the following three statements:

a. The peacetime military draft is great.

b. The good points of the peacetime military draft outweigh the bad points.

c. The peacetime military draft is a necessary evil.

The person who would endorse statement *a* should be judged to disagree strongly with *c* but not *b*. The person who endorses *b* may be judged to disagree strongly with *a*. Thus, if the judged probability of endorsing one statement given another is endorsed is to be used as an indicator of conditional proximity, it could easily lead to violations of the symmetry condition. Furthermore, consider the relationship between endorsing all three statements. A person who endorses statement *a* must also be judged to endorse statement *b;* if this conditional probability of endorsement is to be represented by distance, the distance between *a* and *b* must therefore be small. The same reasoning leads to the conclusion that the distance between *c* and *b* must be small. According to the triangular inequality, then, the distance between *a* and *c* cannot be too large; yet the person who endorses statement *a* will almost *never* be judged to endorse statement *c,* and vice versa.

Conditional proximity measures, in contrast, do yield one check on consistency not present in the analysis of symmetric proximity measures. Consider, for example, measures that indicate object *b* is more psychologically proximal to object *a* than is object *c;* it follows that the distance *ac* must be larger than the distance *ab* in the representation. Further conditional proximity measures could indicate that object *c* is more psychologically proximal to object *b* than is object *a;* it now follows that distance *ab* must be larger than distance *bc* in the representation. Hence *ac* must be larger than *bc,* which in turn implies that object *b* must be seen as more psychologically proximal to object *c* than is object *a.* These implications are illustrated in Figure 4.

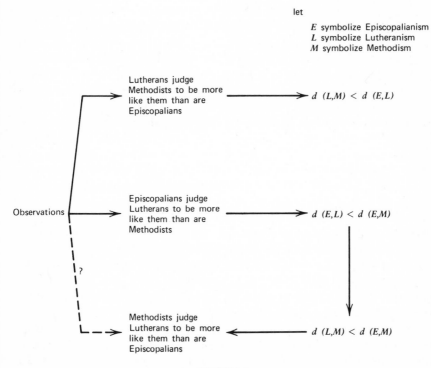

let

E symbolize Episcopalianism
L symbolize Lutheranism
M symbolize Methodism

Lutherans judge Methodists to be more like them than are Episcopalians — $d\ (L,M) < d\ (E,L)$

Observations

Episcopalians judge Lutherans to be more like them than are Methodists — $d\ (E,L) < d\ (E,M)$

Methodists judge Lutherans to be more like them than are Episcopalians — $d\ (L,M) < d\ (E,M)$

FIGURE 4.

4.4 Proximity Techniques as Index Measurement Techniques

Often, there is no concern with the consistency of proximity techniques; instead, the investigator uses a proximity technique as a convenient means of summarizing or depicting his observations—with the hope that the resulting geometric representation will lead to ideas and insights that would not have occurred from looking at the unanalyzed observations. When proximity techniques are used in this manner, they are used as index measurement techniques; although the observations lead to a specifiable representation of the objects whose proximity is evaluated, this representation imposes no constraints on potential observations.

A classic example of the use of proximity techniques for index measurement may be found in Shepard (1963). Shepard used confusion of Morse code signals as proximity measures and then constructed a spatial representation of these measures by use of a computer program he constructed. He analyzed observations collected on both novice Morse code receivers and experienced receivers. In both analyses, the proximity (confusion) measures could be well represented in two dimensions. For both novices and experienced receivers, one of the dimensions could be interpreted as number of components, but the second dimension was different for the two groups; for the novices, the second dimension could be interpreted as "heterogeneity" whereas for the experienced receivers it could be interpreted as being defined by the number of dots versus the number of dashes. Thus, for example, ----- and ..... were located near each other on the second dimension for the novices, but were at opposite ends of the second dimension for the experienced receivers (these two signals being confused quite often by the novices but almost never by the experts). Shepard concluded that the overall pattern of the signal was much more important for the novices than for the experienced receivers—who made confusions on the basis of misperceiving single elements, instead of confusing whole patterns. (The results could further be interpreted in terms of response confusion versus stimulus confusion, or in terms of confusion of Gestalt versus confusion of elements.)

Of course, Shepard did not need to construct a spatial representation in order to reach his conclusion. He could have just looked at his data and seen that the novices tended to confuse signals with similar patterns, whereas the experienced receivers tended to confuse patterns that were alike in all but one element. As Shepard rather convincingly points out, however, discovering the pattern of confusions by looking at the confusion measures themselves is a little difficult; there are 26 letters in the alphabet plus 10 numbers for which there are Morse code signals; hence there are 36 signals and therefore 36 x 36 or 1296 confusion measures. Shepard makes his point by presenting these measures in a square matrix and inviting the reader to analyze their pattern.

The most common proximity technique falling under the heading of index measurement is factor analysis. Factor analysis provides a spatial representation of variables whose proximity is assessed by correlation coefficients. For example, the variables represented might be tests of attitude; these tests are intercorrelated across people and are then represented in a space of k dimensions in such a way that the distances between the points corresponding to the tests represent their intercorrelations. To represent the position of these tests in the k-dimensional space, their projections on k coordinates are assessed. These k coordinates are the *factors* of factor analysis. Furthermore, it is possible to assess each individual's (or observation) "score" on each coordinate (or factor) by combining its score on the variables and the projection of the variables on the coordinates. From these "factor scores" it is possible to *reconstruct* the scores on the initial variables—within a margin of error. Since there will be fewer coordinates than variables (far fewer if the factor analysis is successful), such scores may be a valuable way of characterizing the individuals (or observations). This procedure is used in Section 8.2.

The Geometry of Factor Analysis

(This section may be skipped by the reader lacking the necessary mathematical background without hampering understanding of any later material.) Factor analysis is a metric technique. The correlation between two variables determines the exact distance between their representation in the factor space. To see how this determination is made, consider M variables with N observations on each. Each of the variables may be regarded as defining a point in an N-dimensional space according to the rule that the standard score value of the ith observation (z_{x_i}) is that point's projection on the ith Cartesian coordinate in the space. Each observation then corresponds to a coordinate. And it turns out that each point representing a variable is precisely $\sqrt{N}$ units distance from the origin of that space. By the generalized Pythagorean theorem

$$d^2 (X,0) = \sum_{i=1}^{N} (z_{x_i} - 0)^2 = \sum_{i=1}^{N} z_{x_i}^2 = N.$$

Let N be the "unit of measurement" in the space; the squared distance between two points is now given by

$$d^2 (X, Y) = \sum_{i=1}^{N} (z_{x_i} - z_{y_i})^2 = \sum_{i=1}^{N} z_{x_i}^2 - 2\sum_{i=1}^{N} z_{x_i} z_{y_i} + \sum_{i=1}^{N} z_{y_i}^2$$

$$= N - 2Nr_{xy} = N$$

$$= N2 (1 - r_{xy}).$$

Or, in terms of our unit measurement, $2 (1 - r_{xy})$.

It follows from the law of cosines that $r_{xy} = \cos \theta$, where θ is the angle formed by connecting the two points with the origin.

This geometric interpretation of correlation is presented in Figure 5.

Factor analysis constructs a corresponding space of k instead of N dimensions in which the distances between the variables are more or less preserved. The

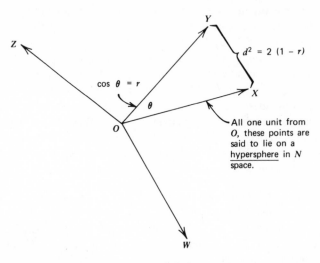

FIGURE 5.

coordinates of this k-dimensional space are the *factors*. The "factor loadings" of the variables are the projections of them on the k dimensions; these projections are, in turn, hypothetical correlation coefficients. The hypothetical score of each observation on these coordinates (the *factor scores*) may be estimated by multiply regressing the factors (coordinates) on the variables (using the hypothetical correlation coefficients). In a variant of factor analysis termed *component analysis*, these factor scores may be obtained directly instead of being estimated.

Factor analysis *can* result in representational measurement instead of index measurement if the investigator examines some consistency criteria (see Section 3.4 for a discussion of the role of the investigator in the distinction between representational and index measurement). Usually, however, it does not. Often a set of variables is intercorrelated and the factor analysis is performed in such a way that the *best* solution, that is, the best estimate of the variables' projection on the factors, is obtained. When you do a factor analysis you get factors.

QUESTIONS

1. In his important work *The Psychology of Personal Constructs,* George Kelly states (p. 307) that "similarity is not just 'similarity' but is similarity with respect to something!" Contrast his view with that of Goodman and present arguments for each (including introspective observation). If Kelly's views are accepted as being correct, what implications do they have for proximity techniques?

2. Devise at least three ways in which the psychological proximity of attitudes might be evaluated.

3. Propose at least two measures that appear to be measures of the psychological proximity of attitudes that may, in fact, be inappropriate and explain why.

4. It was stated in this chapter that it was always possible to construct a nonmetric representation of proximity measures between n objects in a space of $n - 2$ dimensions. Demonstrate that this assertion is true for $n = 3$.

5. The attitude statement "The good points of the peacetime military draft outweigh the bad points" is termed a *monotone* statement because it should be endorsed by anyone who has a certain amount or more of positive attitude toward the draft. In contrast, the statement "The peacetime military draft is a necessary evil" is termed a *nonmonotone* statement because it should be endorsed only by people who have a particular slightly positive attitude toward the draft. Make up five additional monotone attitude statements and five additional nonmonotone attitude statements.

6. Confusion between stimuli can be used as a basis for representing them by magnitude techniques (as described in Chapter II). Confusion can also be used as a basis for representing stimuli by proximity techniques (as described in this chapter). The types of confusion in the two contexts are different. How are they different?

V

Interlocking Techniques

5.1 Introduction

In Chapters II to IV, the techniques presented were used to measure magnitude or proximity of stimuli—crimes, attitude statements, occupations, vocal expressions, religions, and classroom behaviors. All these techniques were based on the responses of people to these stimuli. But the people were not represented in the measures (numerical representations) obtained.

In contrast, the purpose of interlocking techniques is to represent *both* people and stimuli *jointly*—in such a way that order in the representation reflects behavioral domination. For example, an individual judges that a particular beer is too tart; the beer may then be represented above the individual's ideal on a dimension of tartness. Or an individual endorses a monotone attitude statement (see Question No. 5, Chapter IV); the resulting representation places the individual above the statement on a dimension of a favorability toward its subject matter.

There are multidimensional interlocking techniques. But they are rare. Most interlocking techniques are unidimensional; people are represented above or below stimuli on a single dimension depending on their responses to the stimuli. For example, people and arithmetic items may be represented on a scale of arithmetic difficulty in such a way that the individual is placed above the item if and only if the individual passes the item. In the domain of attitude measurement, the stimuli are most often monotone attitude statements or overt behaviors, and individuals are placed above these statements or behaviors if and only if they endorse the statement or engage in the behavior; the most common dimensions are those of positive or negative attitude toward a group or issue.

The basic interlocking technique is known as the *Guttman scalogram technique* because it was first specified in its entirety by Guttman (see Horst, 1941), and it was he who used it in World War II to investigate such diverse topics as enlisted men's attitudes toward officers and fear symptoms in combat (Guttman, 1944, 1950). Although Guttman developed the technique in its explicit form, the basic idea extends at least as far back as Bogardus' (1928) social distance scale, and perhaps farther. The idea is that it may be possible to order certain

44

stimuli in such a way that if an individual dominates a particular stimulus, he will also dominate all the stimuli ordered below that stimulus; also, if he fails to dominate a particular stimulus, he will fail to dominate any of the stimuli above that stimulus in the order. For example, an increasingly difficult series of arithmetic items may be ordered according to their difficulty; if these items form a true Guttman, that is, interlocking, scale, then an individual who passes any given item (meaning he should be represented above it) can be expected to pass all the easier items, and one who fails a given item can be expected to fail all the more difficult ones.

If such an ordering is possible, the result is that people and stimuli are represented in an interlocking order. Each person is represented between two stimuli—the stimulus highest in the order that he dominates and that lowest in the order that he fails to dominate. The question of whether such an inter-locking order is possible is empirical.

Consider, for example, the arithmetic items that are ordered according to increasing difficulty. If individuals' responses to these items can be represented perfectly in an interlocking scale, then each individual can be represented between two items; the individual passes all the items represented below him and fails all those represented above him. Since there are n items, there are only $n + 1$ places in which the individual can be represented, and since each postion corresponds to a particular pattern of passing and failing items, there are only $n + 1$ such patterns.

There are, however, 2^n possible response patterns (patterns of dominating and failing to dominate stimuli). The question of whether there are possible response patterns that do not, in fact, occur is crucial to the question of whether people and stimuli can be represented in an interlocking order. That is, if people and arithmetic items can be represented perfectly by a Guttman scale, there are *at most* $n + 1$ response patterns. If there is no order to the people and the items, all 2^n response patterns may occur. Thus, the hypothesis that the people and items can be represented by a Guttman (interlocking) scale requires that many fewer response patterns occur than could occur. (For $n = 6$, there are only 7 patterns consistent with a Guttman representation, but 64 possible patterns if there is no constraint in the peoples' responses.) As will be discussed in the concluding chapter of this book, it is a general principle that measurement—including index measurement—can occur only in the context in which certain behaviors *could* occur but *do not.*

The actual technique for constructing a Guttman scale—if it exists—is simple. If there are n stimuli, and if there is a clear criterion for ordering an individual above a stimulus (e.g., he passes an arithmetic item, endorses a monotone attitude statement), then the desired ordering of stimuli implies the desired ordering of people, and vice versa. The individual highest in the order dominates all stimuli, hence he should be represented above all stimuli. The individual next highest in the interlocking order dominates all stimuli except the most extreme one; hence he should be represented beneath this stimulus but above all others;

moreover, this stimulus should be represented as highest in the order. Now the individual next highest in the order should dominate all stimuli except the highest and one other; he is now represented as the third highest individual, and this one other stimulus is represented as the second highest stimulus. And so on.

The simplest mechanism for obtaining such interlocking order is to construct a matrix whose rows represent people—or response patterns—and whose columns represent stimuli; a 1 is placed in the cell corresponding to the ith row and jth column if and only if individual i has dominated stimulus j. Such a matrix is represented in part a of Figure 1. It is possible to construct an interlocking scale if and only if the rows and columns of such a matrix can be rearranged so that there is a triangular pattern of 1's in it. The individual who dominates all stimuli should be represented in the first row; the individual who dominates all but one stimulus should be represented in the second row; the individual who dominates all but two stimuli should be represented in the third row, and so on. Then the stimulus represented by the first column is the most extreme stimulus, the stimulus represented by the second column is the next most extreme, and so on. Part b of Figure 1 illustrates the matrix presented in part a with its rows and columns rearranged in such ways as to obtain a triangular pattern. When such a pattern is obtained, the people and stimuli are represented in an interlocking order according to the rule that the person represented by row j is placed between the stimuli represented by columns j and $j-1$.

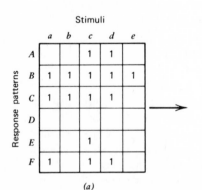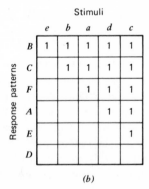

FIGURE 1.

Occasionally, not all $n + 1$ response patterns will be found among an investigator's observations. If some are missing, the procedure outlined above must be modified; there will be fewer rows than columns in the original matrix of observations, and they must be rearranged not to form a perfect triangular pattern of domination but instead to form a quasi-triangular pattern—as illustrated in Figure 2. When there are more stimuli than response patterns, the order of certain stimuli is ambiguous; for example, the order of stimuli e and f in

Figure 2 is not known (if columns e and f were reversed, the same pattern of 1's would be obtained), nor is the order of stimuli c, d, and a.

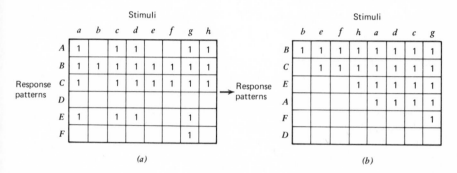

FIGURE 2.

Finally, in actual applications there may be a few deviant response patterns, that is, a few that do not correspond to any of the $n + 1$ required if the behavioral domination is to be represented by a Guttman scale. As was discussed in Section 3.4, the problem is one of determining whether such deviations are caused by observational error or caused by the fact that the behavior observed is basically inconsistent with the proposed representation. There is no easy solution to this problem, and none is proposed in this book (see Section 7.2).

5.2 An Early Example

An enduring interest of social psychologists has been the study of individuals' attitudes toward other people as a function of the ethnic or national group to which these people belong—that is, the study of prejudice. In order to evaluate individuals' prejudices, Bogardus (1925) developed what he termed a *social distance scale*. The idea underlying this scale is that the more prejudiced an individual is against a particular group, the greater the social distance he insists on maintaining between himself and members of that group. For example, if the individual is extremely prejudiced, he may insist that members of that group not even be allowed to visit his country; if he is only slightly prejudiced, he may accept group members as neighbors, but not accept them to close kinship by marriage. Thus, his prejudice is assessed by discovering the degree of social distance an individual places between himself and members of the group against whom he is prejudiced—the greater the distance, the greater the prejudice.

Bogardus developed his social distance scale by asking whether individuals would accept group members as citizens, as neighbors, as fellow club members, and so on. He did not explicitly state the principle of the Guttman scale, but the idea is implicit in his concept of social distance. If the individual would not let a group member come within a certain social distance of him, he should not let the group member come any closer (e.g., if he refuses to grant him citizenship, he should refuse him as a neighbor); furthermore, if the individual allows the group member to come within a certain distance, he should allow him to come within all greater distances (e.g., if he would allow him to become a fellow club member, he should allow him as a visitor to the country). It should then be possible to construct a Guttman scale according to the principle that the ethnic group dominates a certain distance criterion if and only if the individual expressing his prejudice toward that group refuses to allow a group member to come within that distance.

Notice that this example has some rather unusual features. Most often, a Guttman scale represents real people dominating or failing to dominate real stimuli. In this example, the "people" are stereotypes of a single prejudiced judge, and the "stimuli" are hypothetical situations indicative of social distance. These unique features have no bearing on the logic of Guttman scaling (see Section 7.1 of Chapter VII); the Guttman scaling procedure only involves the establishment of an interlocking order between two sets of elements, the nature of these elements being irrelevant to the measurement procedure.

Notice that the Bogardus procedure involves construction of a separate Guttman scale representing the prejudice of each individual; if the order of hypothetical situations on these scales is the same from individual to individual, then there is very strong evidence for Bogardus' concept of social distance. In general, the order is the same, but there are interesting cultural differences (see Triandis & Triandis, 1965).

Table 1 presents the responses of a single subject to questions concerning social distance (Bogardus, 1925, p. 300). The way in which these questions were presented to the subject is identical to the format of Table 1; the X's in Table 1 indicate the X's as placed by the subject.

The questions in Table 1 are phrased both in terms of exclusion and inclusion; that is, the most extreme question is phrased in terms of exclusion ("would exclude from my country"), and the other questions are phrased in terms of inclusion ("to my club as personal chums"). To be consistent with the concept of social distances outlined in this chapter, all items should be scored in terms of exclusion; thus, when the individual whose responses are illustrated in Table 1 does not place an X indicating he would admit certain group members to certain hypothetical situations, he is then scored as excluding them. The rows and columns of Table 1 so scored can be rearranged in order to form a quasi-triangular pattern that reflects the Guttman scale. This rearrangement is presented in Table 2.

Notice that the pattern in Table 2 is perfect. There is not a single instance of a group member being excluded from one situation and then not being excluded from all situations involving closer social distance. There are, however, some ambiguities in the order of exclusion—just as there were ambiguities in Figure 2.

Table 1   Document 1: Social Distances

According to my first feeling reactions I would willingly admit members of each race (as a class, and not the best I have known, nor the worst members) to one or more of the classifications under which I have placed a cross(X).

	7 / 1 To close kinship by marriage	6 / 2 To my club as personal chums	5 / 3 To my street as neighbors	4 / 4 To employment in my occupation in my country	3 / 5 To citizenship in my country	2 / 6 As visitors only to my country	1 / 7 Would exclude from my country
Armenians						X	
Bulgarians						X	
Canadians	X	X	X	X	X		
Chinese						X	
Czecho-Slovaks						X	
Danes				X	X		
Dutch				X	X		
English	X	X	X	X	X		
French	X	X	X	X	X		
French-Canadians	X	X	X	X	X		
Finns				X	X		
Germans	X	X	X	X	X		
Greeks							X
Hindus							X
Hungarians						X	
Indians (Amer.)				X	X		
Irish	X	X	X	X	X		
Italians				X	X		
Japanese							X
Jew-German						X	
Jew-Russian						X	
Koreans							X
Mexicans						X	
Mulattos							X
Negroes							X
Norwegians	X	X	X	X	X		
Portugese						X	
Filipinos						X	
Poles						X	
Roumanians	X	X	X	X	X		
Russians						X	
Serbo-Croatians						X	
Scotch	X	X	X	X	X		
Scotch-Irish	X	X	X	X	X		
Spanish						X	
Syrians							X
Swedish				X	X		
Turks							X
Welch	X	X	X	X	X		

1. Your father's races   English
2. Your mother's races   Scotch-Irish

Table 2

	Would exclude from my country	Would not allow to stay in my country for any length of time	Would not allow citizenship in my country	Would not allow employment in my occupation in my country	Would not allow on my street as neighbors	Would not have in my club as personal chums	Would not allow into kinship by marriage
Greeks	X	X	X	X	X	X	X
Hindus	X	X	X	X	X	X	X
Japanese	X	X	X	X	X	X	X
Koreans	X	X	X	X	X	X	X
Mulattos	X	X	X	X	X	X	X
Negroes	X	X	X	X	X	X	X
Syrians	X	X	X	X	X	X	X
Turks	X	X	X	X	X	X	X
Armenians		X	X	X	X	X	X
Bulgarians		X	X	X	X	X	X
Chinese		X	X	X	X	X	X
Czecho-Slovaks		X	X	X	X	X	X
Hungarians		X	X	X	X	X	X
Jew-Germans		X	X	X	X	X	X
Jew-Russians		X	X	X	X	X	X
Mexicans		X	X	X	X	X	X
Portugese		X	X	X	X	X	X
Filipinos		X	X	X	X	X	X
Poles		X	X	X	X	X	X
Russians		X	X	X	X	X	X
Serbo-Croatians		X	X	X	X	X	X
Spanish		X	X	X	X	X	X
Danes					X	X	X
Dutch					X	X	X
Finns					X	X	X
Indians (Amer.)					X	X	X
Italians					X	X	X
Swedish					X	X	X
Canadians							
English							
French							
French-Canadians							
Germans							
Irish							
Norwegians							
Roumanians							
Scotch							
Scotch-Irish							
Welch							

The situations of employment, citizenship, and visiting cannot be ordered on the basis of the observations; instead they have been ordered in a way that seemed most reasonable according to their content; furthermore, the situations of marriage, club membership, and neighborhood integration also cannot be ordered. Bogardus reports, however, that marriage is the single best indicator of any prejudice at all. The person who states that he would admit a group member to close kinship by marriage will generally include group members in all situations.

The content of this example is of some interest. The observations were collected in 1925, and observations of this sort have often been collected from then until the time of publication of this book—a recent study being reported by Karlins, Coffman, and Walters (1969). Generally, over the course of the last 45 years, college students have become less prejudiced, and especially less prejudiced toward nonwhite groups with whom they have had contact. For example, the early studies show very strong prejudice against Negroes, Chinese, and Japanese (Katz & Braly, 1933). These prejudices appear to have diminished over time—to the point where the study of Karlins, Coffman, and Walters reports that the stereotypes of Japanese are more favorable than are stereotypes of Americans! It must be kept in mind, however, that the subjects in these studies are college students, not the "general public." Moreover, it must be remembered that many of the people in United States' society in the 1970s with the most power are those who were college students during the 1930s.

(One consistent finding of these studies deserves special mention—although it is not of central importance. Throughout the 45-year period, the subjects have consistently indicated prejudice against Turks. In fact, Turks are often found at the very bottom of the numerical scale that the investigator presents to summarize his observations. Why do the subjects show more prejudice against Turks than against other national or ethnic groups? Turkey is a NATO ally of the United States; Turks fought beside United States troops in Korea; and several generations have passed since Turkey subjugated any surrounding countries. This finding of prejudice against Turks is especially interesting in light of the twin finding that many of the subjects in these studies disclaim any knowledge of what Turks are like, and the subjects who are willing to describe Turks disagree more about the characteristics of Turks than about those of any other group! See Karlins, Coffman, and Walters, 1969, p. 9, for summary of these findings.)

Finally, it should be noted that this example concerns people's statements about exclusion of other people, not actual exclusion. In a classic and provocative study by LaPiere (1934), the discovery was made that people are often *less* prejudiced in their actions than in their words. LaPiere traveled around the country with a Chinese couple. When he asked motel and hotel owners over the phone or by letter whether they would accommodate Chinese couples, he found many who said they would not. When, however, the couple actually appeared at motels and hotels, they were almost never refused service.

Noting the sort of discrepancy LaPiere discovered, some writers will make a distinction between what they term "attitude" and what they term "behavior." Such a distinction implies a theoretical position involving attitude—specifically, that it is something other than overt behavior. Since this position is not necessary, the distinction made in this book will be between verbal attitude and nonverbal attitude (e.g., as expressed by accepting or rejecting people as motel clients).

There is no reason that an attempt could not be made to construct a Guttman scale of social distance based on real inclusion and exclusion instead of on statements about inclusion and exclusion. Again, the question of whether such a scale could be constructed is empirical; it can be constructed if and only if the constraints imposed by the technique are satisfied by the observations.

5.3 Consistency Checks

The basic test of the consistency of the Guttman scalogram technique is based on the possibility of actually constructing the scale—by using the procedure outlined in Section 5.1 or some similar algorithm. If it is possible to construct the interlocking order, then the constraints imposed by the technique are satisfied. If it is not possible to construct the interlocking order, then there is at least one violation of these constraints. Thus, the technique will be consistent if and only if it is possible to construct the interlocking order.

Another method for checking the consistency of the scalogram analysis involves examining each pair of stimuli. If each pair of stimuli may be ordered, then the entire set may be ordered. And a pair of stimuli (j, k) may be ordered if and only if there are no two response patterns among the observations that yield contrary implications about the order; that is, the observations must not contain *both* a response pattern in which j is dominated and k is not and a response pattern in which k is dominated and j is not. This constraint is illustrated in Figure 3.

There is, as was mentioned earlier, the question of how much inconsistency will be tolerated before the decision is made that a set of observations cannot be represented by an interlocking order. Although there is no definite answer to this question, one word of caution is necessary. *If the number of observations collected is small, then it is often possible to construct something that looks like a Guttman scale—even if the response patterns are generated randomly.*

Consider, for example, sampling 20 observations of domination of two stimuli *a* and *b* from a population in which there is *no* interlocking pattern of people and stimuli. Consider, also, that all four responses to these two stimuli are equally likely in the population; that is, 25 percent of the people dominate both *a* and *b*, 25 percent dominate *a* but not *b*, 25 percent dominate *b* but not *a*, and 25 percent dominate neither. It would not be at all unlikely to obtain a

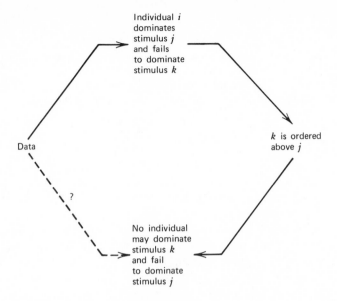

FIGURE 3.

sample in which 7 people dominate both *a* and *b,* 2 people dominate *a* alone, 6 people dominate *b* alone, and 5 people fail to dominate either.[1] Then 90 percent (18 of 20) of the response patterns conform to a Guttman scale in which *a* is ordered above *b*. Moreover, it is necessary to regard only 2 of the 40 actual responses to be in error in order to have a perfect Guttman scale. (The people who dominated *a* should have dominated *b* also.)

One minus the proportion of responses that must be changed in order to obtain a perfect scale is sometimes termed a *coefficient of reproducibility*. In this example, this coefficient is .95, which sounds impressive. As illustrated by this example, however, high values of this coefficient can often be misleading. In fact, Rutherford, Morrison, and Campbell (1972) found that when they *randomly* generated 100 responses to 6 stimuli, they obtained a coefficient of reproducibility of .89 (although their results did not "look like" a Guttman scale). The problem is that the order of the stimuli is determined *after* collecting the observations, and hence "capitalization on chance" is bound to occur. If the order is specified a priori, there is no such problem.

---

[1] The Pearson chi-square value for testing the hypothesis that all response patterns are equally likely is 2.80. The value needed to reject this hypothesis at the .05 level is 7.81 (df. = 3).

5.4 Guttman Scaling Where Direction of Domination Is Unknown

Schubert (1961) and Spaeth (1965) have presented an array of observations of Supreme Court voting that indicate that judges and cases can be represented by an interlocking order. If a judge votes on the liberal (conservative) side in one case, he votes on the liberal (conservative) side of all cases requiring less liberalism (conservatism). There are few inconsistencies in the data; for example, Spaeth (1965, p. 298) shows that of 230 votes on cases involving economic liberalism in 1962, there were only 15 votes that were inconsistent with the interlocking order he developed. (Actually, Spaeth found a distinction between liberalism as applied to economics and liberalism as applied to civil rights problems. Although the judges were not ordered identically on both dimensions, there was a high intercorrelation between their ranking; the interested reader is referred to Spaeth's article.)

Suppose now that Schubert and Spaeth had not known which vote on a given case indicated that the judge should be represented on the liberal side of that case. The observations concern whether a particular judge voted for one side or the other in a particular case; if the investigator analyzing these votes had no idea whether voting for a particular side was voting on the liberal or conservative side, he could not determine whether the judge dominated or failed to dominate the case. Is Guttman scaling possible in such a situation?

The answer is yes. The possibility of such scaling rests on the fact that the only two response patterns that are in complete disagreement are those of the people who should be represented at the two extremes of the dimension. See Figures 1 and 2.

If the observations can be represented by a Guttman scale, then there will be one and only one such pair of response patterns. Everyone but the least extreme subject[2] will dominate the least extreme stimulus, and everyone but the most extreme subject will fail to dominate the most extreme stimulus; hence, all these nonextreme people will respond in the same way to the least extreme stimulus (i.e., in the same way that the most extreme individual responds—by dominating it), and they will respond in the same way to the most extreme stimulus (i.e., in the same way the least extreme individual responds—by failing to dominate it). Only the two extreme people have opposite response patterns.

Dominating a stimulus involves responding to it in the same way that the most extreme individual responds to it. If the pattern of domination can be represented by a true Guttman scale, this most extreme individual will be one member of that pair of individuals whose response patterns are completely different. If, then, a true Guttman scale representation is possible, there will be precisely one such pair, and domination of a stimulus can be identified as responding to it in the same way as does one of the members of this pair. Which

---

[2] No differentiation is made between people with the same response pattern; hence, we refer to such people as if they constituted a single individual, for example, "the" extreme individual.

member? It doesn't matter, since the same interlocking order will be obtained. (Notice how, in the example of Supreme Court voting, domination could be defined either in terms of voting on the liberal side of an issue or in terms of voting on the conservative side.)

This procedure is described in greater detail in Dawes and Winter (1969).

When Dawes first suggested that domination could be defined as agreeing with an extreme response pattern (see Coombs, 1964, p. 270), the objection was raised that both extreme patterns might not happen to be in an investigator's sample, and hence it would not be possible to identify them. The objection seemed reasonable, but on closer examination, it isn't. Suppose, for example, that the individual who dominates all stimuli is not present in the sample. Then there will be no individual who dominates the most extreme stimulus, and hence all individuals will respond in the same way to that stimulus; such a stimulus, since it doesn't differentiate between individuals, would be removed from further consideration in constructing the scale. Then, if there is someone who dominates the next most extreme stimulus, he automatically becomes the most extreme individual; if, however, there is no such person, then once again everyone responds in the same way to the next most extreme stimulus—and it too is removed from consideration. The process is continued until an extreme individual is obtained. The same argument leads to the conclusion that stimuli dominated by all individuals will be removed until there is some individual who fails to dominate any stimulus. Hence, once stimuli to which everyone responds in the same way are removed from the sample, it *must* contain both the individual who dominates all the remaining stimuli and the individual who fails to dominate any.

A slightly different method for constructing a Guttman scale when direction of domination is unknown was presented by Dawes, Brown, and Kaplan (1965). Their observations were of Supreme Court justices, and will be used here to illustrate the technique outlined above. First, they selected 25 cases from the year 1961.

"The selection was subject to the constraint that the cases be decided upon a point of law; that is, the decision was neither a decision of whether the Supreme Court had proper jurisdiction, nor a decision of whether proper procedure was followed in administering an unchallenged law. Of the 25 cases, there was a unanimous decision on 10, and they were consequently dropped from consideration. The remaining 15 were divided into seven that concerned business matters and eight that concerned civil rights."[3]

The eight cases concerning civil rights are presented in Figure 4; a D in this figure indicates that the judge represented in the row dissented from the majority opinion concerning the case represented in the column.

---

[3]This division was made prior to any attempt to construct a Guttman scale.

		Cases[a]							
		1	2	3	4	5	6	7	8
	Warren	D	D	D				D	D
	Frankfurter						D		
	Black	D	D	D		D		D	D
	Douglas	D	D	D		D		D	D
Judges	Clark				D		D		
	Harlan						D		
	Brennan	D	D	D				D	D
	Whittaker				D		D		
	Stewart								

FIGURE 4.

First, it should be noted that Black and Douglas have the same response pattern, Warren and Brennan have the same response pattern, Frankfurter and Harlan have the same response pattern, and Whittaker and Clark have the same response pattern; hence, no distinction is made between these judges. Furthermore, the votes on cases 1, 2, 3, 7, and 8 are identical, and hence these cases can be treated as constituting a single stimulus. The observations appropriately collapsed are presented in Figure 5.

As required by the method outlined in this section, there is one and only one pair of response patterns that is completely different. That pair consists of the response patterns of Black and Douglas on the one hand and Whittaker and Clark on the other. Following the procedure, agreement with Black and Douglas

		Cases			
		1, 2, 3, 7, 8	4	5	6
	Warren and Brennan	D			
	Frankfurter and Harlan				D
Judges	Black and Douglas	D		D	
	Whittaker and Clark		D		D
	Stewart				

FIGURE 5.

[a]Communist Party v. U.S. Subversive Activities Control Board 81 SC 1357; Scales v. U.S. 81 SC 1469; Gori v. U.S. 81 SC 1523; Reck v. Pate 81 SC 1541; U.S. v. Shimer 81 SC 1554; Deutch v. U.S. 81 SC 1587; Wilkenson v. U.S. 81 SC 567; Brandon v. U.S. 81 SC 584.

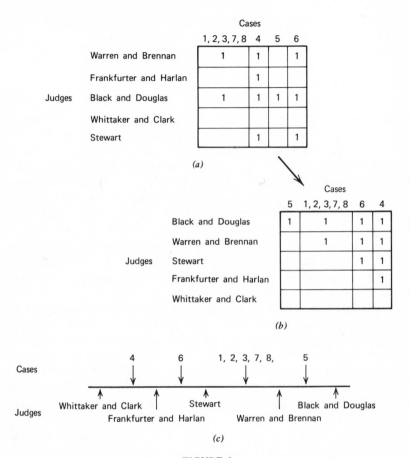

FIGURE 6.

is defined as dominating the case. Figure 6*a* illustrates the pattern of domination; in Figure 6*b* the rows and columns have been rearranged in order to form the triangular pattern that yields the desired interlocking order of judges and cases; Figure 6*c* provides a spatial representation of the resulting order. Since domination was defined as agreeing with Black and Douglas, the dimension is most readily interpreted as one of liberalism, where dominating (i.e., being on the liberal side) involves voting with the majority in cases 4 and 6 and dissenting in cases 1, 2, 3, 7, 8, and 5. The order of the judges on this dimension corresponds to the order found by both Schubert and Spaeth. It is of some interest to note that Stewart, the judge in the middle, voted with the majority on every case.

The caution expressed at the end of Section 5.3 is also applicable to this technique—perhaps even more applicable. Here the investigator decides not only the order of the stimuli after looking at his observations, but the direction of domination as well. The degree to which this technique will generate something approximating a Guttman scale in the absence of any real constraint in the population from which observations are sampled is not yet known, but certainly there is a great deal of opportunity for "capitalization on chance."

5.5 A Generalization

People and stimuli (or any two appropriate sets) may be represented in more than one dimension. In order to establish such a multidimensional representation, the rule by which an individual is regarded as dominating a stimulus must be specified—and tested for consistency. For example, one possible rule is a *linear* one: the observation that an individual dominates a stimulus is represented by requiring that the weighted sum of the coordinates of the point representing the individual be larger than the corresponding weighted sum of the coordinates of the point representing the stimulus. For example, an individual may dominate the entrance requirements of a given university if the weighted sum of his high school grade point average, college aptitude scores, and letter of recommendation ratings is greater than the weighted sum of these variables required by the admissions standards of the university.

Another possible rule is a *conjunctive* one: domination is defined by requiring that *all* the coordinates of the points representing the individual be greater than the corresponding coordinates of the points representing the stimulus. For example, a graduate school may require minimal scores on the Graduate Record Examination (GRE), and a minimal grade point average (GPA); an individual will meet the standards of such a graduate school if and only if his GRE scores are higher than the minimal requirements and his grades yield a GPA higher than the minimum.

Yet another possible rule is a *disjunctive* one: an individual is regarded as dominating a stimulus if and only if *at least one* of the coordinates of the points representing the individual is greater than the corresponding coordinate of the

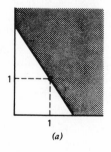 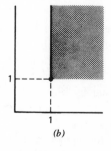 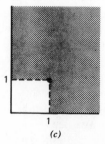

(a)   (b)   (c)

FIGURE 7.

point representing the stimulus. For example, a rookie trying out for a professional football team may dominate the standards of the team if *either* his passing ability, *or* his kicking ability, *or* his defensive ability, and so on, is great enough that he can serve as a specialist in one of these capacities for the team. For a discussion of these three different types of rules—and particularly as they apply to college selections—see Dawes (1964).

These three rules are not the only possible ones. In fact, there is an infinite variety of possible rules—one corresponding to each way it is possible to define an order between two points in a multidimensional space. Nevertheless, these three types of rules are the most common. Figure 7 illustrates them; in this figure, the shaded area indicates points represented in two dimensions that would dominate the point with coordinates (1, 1) according to the three types of rules; Figure 7a illustrates a linear rule, Figure 7b illustrates a conjunctive rule, and Figure 7c illustrates a disjunctive rule.

It should be emphasized that the choice of the rule for domination is not arbitrary, but instead certain sets of response patterns determine which rule is best—that is, which representation is most consistent with the observations. For a discussion of these rules, see Coombs (1964, Chapter 12).

QUESTIONS

1. Bogardus allowed the order of his questions on the *Social Distance* questionnaire (Table 1) to correspond to the order of the Guttman scale. Discuss problems that might result.
2. The observations in Table 1 were altered so that each response indicated exclusion; instead, alter the entries so that each response indicates inclusion, and use the algorithm presented in Section 5.1 to obtain the Guttman scale.
3. Apply the Dawes-Winter algorithm presented in Section 5.4 to the data presented in Table 1; that is, suppose that the respondent indicated whether he would treat each group differently from or the same as the majority of other groups, instead of indicating whether he would exclude it from a given situation. First, however, change the "as visitors only" question to "not for any length of time." What is the problem with the "as visitors only" wording as used by Bogardus?
4. In Section 5.5 it was asserted that the same interlocking order of people and stimuli could be obtained if domination were identified with responding in the same way as the least extreme individual instead of responding in the same way as the most extreme individual. Demonstrate that this assertion is correct for the hypothetical observations presented in Figure 2.
5. After conversation with friends, construct a social distance scale of *overt behaviors* that you think might satisfy the requirements of a Guttman scale. Then observe additional people and see if the constraints imposed by this interlocking order technique are satisfied.

VI

Unfolding Techniques

6.1 Introduction

In 1932, Likert gave the following advice about choosing appropriate statements to form an attitude scale (1932, p. 44):

"Each statement should be of such a nature that persons with different points of view, so far as a particular attitude is concerned, will respond to it different-ly."

In order to select such statements, it is necessary to determine which people have different points of view and which have similar ones. How is this determination made? Usually by observing people's responses to attitude statements—either by their endorsement of such statements (e.g., "I agree with what he said") or by their emission of such statements (e.g., "cleaniness is next to a hand-washing compulsion"). Thus, the appropriateness of an attitude statement is determined by observing the attitudes of people who respond to it, but their attitudes are determined by observing their responses to attitude statements. Is such a procedure circular? Is it perhaps not necessary to assess an individual's attitude by some means other than the statements he endorses in order to obtain appropriate statements?

The answer is no. The procedure is no more circular than is the Guttman scalogram procedure—in which the appropriateness of a stimulus is determined by the position of people who surpass or endorse it, and their location is determined by the stimuli they surpass. (For example, the difficulty of an arithmetic item is assessed by the arithmetic ability of those who pass or fail it, although their ability is assessed by the items they pass or fail.)

In order to understand this lack of circularity, consider six items that can be represented on a liberal-conservative dimension and a number of people who are responding to these items purely in terms of the degree to which they express a liberal versus a conservative philosophy; consider, also, that each individual is asked to endorse the three statements with which he is in greatest agreement. The most liberal individuals will endorse the three most liberal statements; the

(a)

	a	b	c	d	e	f
A		1			1	1
B	1				1	1
C	1		1	1		
D	1		1			1

Most liberal (top) … Least liberal (bottom)

(b)

	Liberal			Conservative		
	d	c	a	f	e	b
C	1	1	1			
D		1	1	1		
B			1	1	1	
A				1	1	1

FIGURE 1.

next most liberal individuals will not endorse the most liberal statement but will endorse the two next to it and the fourth most liberal; and so on. The resulting *endorsement pattern* is presented in Figure 1*b*, a "one" indicating an endorsement. (All identical endorsement patterns are represented by a single row.)

Notice that if the investigator obtaining endorsement did not know prior to collecting his observations that individuals and stimuli could be represented on a liberal-conservative dimension, he might initially order the stimuli in a random manner and obtain the pattern illustrated in Figure 1*a*. He could then rearrange the rows and columns of his response matrix to obtain the *parallelogram* pattern presented in Figure 1*b*—just as the rows and columns of Figure 1 in Chapter V were rearranged to form a triangular pattern. Thus the *pattern* of responses yields a joint ordering of people and stimuli, just as it did in Guttman scalogram analysis; the difference is that the responses here are interpreted in terms of (i.e., are represented by) proximity, rather than order.

The purpose of unfolding techniques is to represent people and stimuli *jointly* in a space in such a way that the relative distances between the points reflect the psychological proximity of the stimuli to the people, or to their ideals. For example, a technique may be meant to reflect preferences for beer; then, the point representing beer j will be closer to the point representing an individual i's ideal beer than is the point representing beer k if and only if the individual prefers beer j to beer k. Or a technique may be meant to reflect endorsement of nonmonotone attitude statements; here, the point representing statement j will be closer to the point representing individual i than is the point representing statement k whenever the individual endorses statement j and rejects statement k.

Unfolding techniques combine the basic ideas of proximity techniques and interlocking techniques. Psychological proximity is represented, and the proximity is that between people and stimuli instead of between stimuli alone. And as pointed out in Section 5.2 of the preceding chapter, techniques designed to measure people and stimuli jointly can be applied to any pairs of distinct sets.

6.2 Unidimensional Unfolding

The original unfolding technique was developed by Coombs (1950) and has come to be known as *the* unfolding technique. It is a technique designed to construct *a single dimension* representing the proximity of stimuli to a set of individuals. For example, the observations might consist of students' rank orders of expected grades in a course, or of respondents' rank orders of preference for a set of nonmonotone attitude statements expressing political philosophy, or—in the example to be discussed in Section 6.3—of women's rank order preference for the number of children they want in their families. It is natural in these examples to conceptualize the stimuli as lying on a single dimension—*A-F*, left-wing to right-wing, one through many—and to conceptualize people's expectations or preferences as corresponding to the proximity of the stimuli on the dimension to an ideal preference or expectation. The technique begins with these observations of psychological proximity of stimuli to people and constructs a unidimensional representation so that stimulus *j* is closer on the dimension to individual *i* than is stimulus *k* if and only if it is more proximal psychologically; or the technique may demonstrate that such a representation is impossible.

Certain terms must now be introduced in order to be consistent with Coombs' presentation of his technique. On the basis of the assessment of the psychological proximity of each stimulus to each subject, the rank order of the proximity of all stimuli to a single subject *i* can often be obtained (in fact, in many situations the basic observations may consist of the subject's own ranking of the stimuli); this rank order for subject *i* is termed subject *i*'s *I-scale*. Furthermore, if the technique is successfully applied, the rank order of the stimuli on the common dimension is termed a *J-scale*. (*I* and *J* stand for "individual" and "joint" respectively.) The purpose of the technique can now be stated as that of demonstrating how a set of *I*-scales can—or cannot—be represented by points on a *J*-scale.

The technique is illustrated in Figure 2. The letters on the horizontal line in the figure indicate where certain hypothetical stimuli are represented. The two arrows indicate places where hypothetical people might be represented. Given the representation of the person, it is possible to determine the rank order of the distances of the stimuli from that point—the rank order that should correspond to the individual's *I*-scale. This rank can, in fact, be obtained by "folding" the *J*-scale about the point representing the individual. Thus the name "*unfolding*"; the *I*-scales correspond to the *J*-scale folded about the point representing the individual, and these *I*-scales must be unfolded into the common *J*-scale. Figure 2 illustrates both folding and unfolding. The distance of the stimuli from I_1 and I_2 is represented on the lines above I_1 and I_2; the dotted lines indicate how these distances are obtained by folding the underlying scale about I_1 and I_2; the problem is to unfold these distances to obtain the underlying dimension.

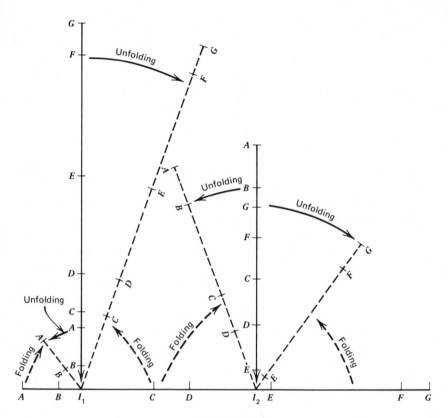

FIGURE 2.

The I-scale of the individual represented by the point labeled I_1 in Figure 2 would be $BACDEFG$; this I-scale corresponds to the distances of those stimuli from I_1. The I-scale of the individual represented by the point labeled I_2 would be $EDCFGBA$—the rank order of the distances of the stimuli from I_2. The distances on each side of I_1 and I_2 are indicated by the dotted lines; the interlocking of these distances determines the final rank order, and hence the J-scale.

The actual technique for unfolding is conceptually simple; its application, however, is often complex because certain crucial I-scales may not be found among the observations that an investigator wishes to unfold, or some I-scales may be inconsistent with one another. If, however, all permissible I-scales are found among the observations, and if there is no inconsistency, then unfolding can be accomplished through the principles outlined in Section 5.4 of the previous chapter. First, the rank order of the stimuli on the dimension is determined by finding which two I-scales are mirror images of each other; the only two I-scales that can be mirror images of each other are those that correspond to the individuals represented on the two extremes of the dimension, and the order of the stimuli on the J-scale is identical to the order on their I-scales. See Figure 2.

Once the order of the stimuli on the dimension has been determined, unfolding is accomplished by constructing a Guttman scale interlocking individuals and midpoints of stimuli; suppose stimulus β is ordered above stimulus α on the J-scale; then if α is more proximal to individual i than is β, individual i should be represented below the midpoint between α and β; conversely, if β is more proximal to individual i than is α individual i should be represented above the midpoint between α and β. The I-scale of each individual indicates which midpoints he should be represented above and which midpoints he should be represented below. Hence, the unidimensional representation required by Coombs' unfolding technique is obtained by constructing a Guttman scale of individuals and midpoints.

Moreover, the order of midpoints often yields some information about relative distances on the J-scale. For example, suppose four stimuli lie on the J-scale in the order a, b, c, d. The first midpoint of these stimuli is of necessity the ab midpoint, and the second must of necessity be the ac midpoint. The third, however, may be either the bc midpoint or the ad midpoint—while the last two midpoints must be the bd and cd midpoints in that order. Suppose now the ad midpoint precedes the bc midpoint. The distance from a to the ad midpoint is the distance from a to d divided by 2, but the distance from a to the bc midpoint is equal to the distance from a to b plus half the distance from b to c. Hence, since the ad midpoint precedes the bc midpoint,

$$\frac{d\,(a,\,d)}{2} < d\,(a,\,b) + \frac{d\,(b,\,c)}{2}\,.$$

Multiplying both sides of this inequality by 2 yields

$$d\,(a,\,d) < 2d\,(a,\,b) + d\,(b,\,c)\,,$$

since $d\,(a,\,d) = d\,(a,\,c) + d\,(c,\,d)$, the inequality becomes

$$d\,(a,\,c) + d\,(c,\,d) < 2d\,(a,\,b) + d\,(b,\,c)\,.$$

But since $d\,(b,\,c) + d\,(a,\,c) - d\,(a,\,b)$, it becomes

$$d\,(a,\,c) + d\,(c,\,d) < 2d\,(a,\,b) + d\,(a,\,c) - d\,(a,\,b) = d\,(a,\,b) + d\,(a,\,c).$$

Finally, subtracting $d\,(a,\,c)$ from both sides of the inequality yields

$$d\,(c,\,d) < d\,(a,\,b)\,.$$

This implication about distance is illustrated in Figure 3a, and the implication following from the reverse order of the ad and bc midpoints is illustrated in part b.

All information about relative distances that can be inferred from the observations is obtained by examining all sets of four stimuli and observing whether

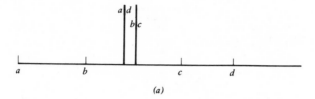

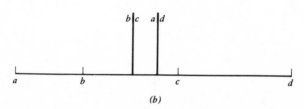

FIGURE 3.

the midpoint between the two outside stimuli (e.g., a, d) precedes the midpoint between the two inside stimuli (e.g., b, c), or whether the midpoints are in reverse order. That is, if the order of the stimuli is a, b, c, d, then the existence of the I-scale $bcda$ implies that the ad midpoint precedes the bc midpoint, while the existence of the I-scale $cbad$ implies that the bc midpoint precedes the ad one.

6.3 Consistency Checks

The easiest way to understand the consistency checks for the unfolding techniques is to conceptualize them in terms of Guttman scaling individuals and midpoints between stimuli. If there are n stimuli, there are $(n^2 - n)/2$ midpoints.[1] Since these midpoints correspond to stimuli with which people are interlocked, there are only $((n^2 - n)/2) + 1$ admissible I-scales. Since, however, an I-scale is a rank ordering of the n stimuli, there are $n!$ possible I-scales. For example, if there are 8 stimuli, there are 28 midpoints hypothesized by the unfolding technique, and hence only 29 different I-scales; there are, however, 40,320 *possible* I-scales. Once again, the question of whether there are possible observa-

---

[1] There are n^2 ordered pairs of n stimuli; n of these pairs consist of a stimulus paired with itself, which does not correspond to a midpoint; furthermore, each midpoint corresponds to two ordered pairs—for example, (a, b) and (b, a); hence, once n is subtracted from n^2 and the result is divided by two, the number of midpoints is obtained.

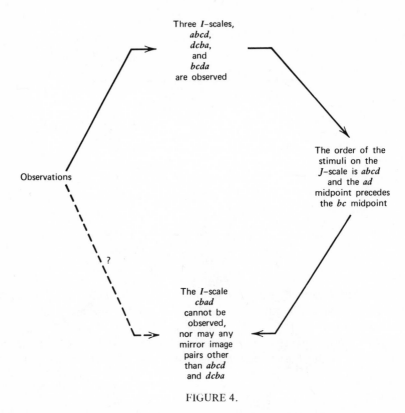

FIGURE 4.

tions that do not in fact occur is crucial to the question of whether observations can be represented by a measurement technique.

The basic test of the consistency of the present technique is based on the possibility of actually constructing the interlocking order of people and midpoints. (See Section 5.1.) Also, in parallel with the pairwise consistency test presented in Section 5.3, it is possible to check the pairwise consistency of midpoints. Again, let four stimuli be represented in the order *a, b, c, d* on the *J*-scale; if an individual prefers *d* to *a* (i.e., must be represented above the *ad* midpoint) but does not prefer *c* to *b* (i.e., must be ordered below the *bc* midpoint), then there should be no individual who prefers *c* to *b* but who does not prefer *d* to *a*. This pairwise constraint is illustrated in Figure 4.

The question of whether it is possible to construct a *J*-scale by the unfolding technique was used as an independent variable in a study by Runkel (1956). He reasoned that two people who respond to stimuli as if they lie on the same dimension will communicate more effectively than will two people who do not—and, more specifically, two people whose preferences can be represented by folding a common *J*-scale at two different points will communicate more effectively than will two people whose preferences cannot be represented in this manner. His example is that of a clothing salesman and customer communicating about suits (1956, pp. 180-181).

"Now let us suppose that person B is communicating with person A about a set of stimuli. Suppose that a clothing salesman is communicating with a customer about suits. 'Try on this size 40,' the salesman suggests. 'Not quite right? Well, let's try a size 42. There, that looks just fine, doesn't it? You'd like to try a size 44? All right, here you are. Yes, I agree, this one is a little too large. The size 42 is just right for you.'

"Let us now ask the customer what the salesman would say about a size 38 or a size 36, or about a size 46 or a size 48. Obviously, the customer can predict very well what sizes the salesman would consider too small and too large. The point is that in providing the customer with an attribute in terms of which his judgments are being made, the salesman is giving the customer his opinions about stimuli which are not mentioned explicitly. From a sample of observed stimuli, the customer gets information about other stimuli which can be judged according to the same attribute as that underlying the judgments among the sampled stimuli. The important qualification here is that both communicators must be making their judgments, and interpreting the communication which occurs, according to the same attribute. If this is the case, each person can make correct predictions about responses the other would make to stimuli not yet communicated about explicitly.

"But the customer might be purchasing a suit to wear to a fancy-dress ball, and the order of sizes might not be at all the order in which he judges how funny the suits are. If the customer with such a purpose does not let the salesman know what attribute is underlying his judgments, we can only feel sorry for the salesman when we imagine the communication which might take place."

What Runkel did was to assess whether two individuals could be viewing stimuli along the same dimensions but from different points by having these individuals indicate their preference for the stimuli. Such an assessment is possible because in addition to the constraints previously mentioned there are constraints between pairs of *I*-scales. Certain pairs cannot be represented as points on the same *J*-scale. For example, the *I*-scale *ABCDE* and the *I*-scale *CEDAB* cannot be so represented.

It is important to note here that two *I*-scales can be incompatible in the sense that they cannot be represented by points on the same *J*-scale; the fact that two *I*-scales are not incompatible (i.e., are compatible) does not, however, imply that they should be represented by points on the same *J*-scale—that is, that the preferences they represent were generated by people having different ideals but viewing the stimuli in a similar manner. Thus, the technique Runkel employed could lead to the conclusion that two people *cannot* be viewing stimuli as lying on the same dimension, but it does not lead to the conclusion that they *are*.

Runkel used his technique to study communication between teachers and students in sections of a large introductory psychology class. Both students and teachers were asked to indicate their preferences for five statements concerning psychology, and it was determined whether or not these preferences could be represented by different points on the same *J*-scale. Runkel's hypothesis was that if they could not, then the students and teacher must be viewing the statements according to different dimensions, and hence should have difficulty in communication in the psychology class; he evaluated communication between student and teacher by the student's grades on section quizzes. The five statements were:

1. The conditions of living in the United States tend to narrow the range of things we are able to decide to do, think about, etc.
2. People who have a firm moral code are in general better adjusted than those who have not.
3. The biggest weakness of present-day psychology is that it is too theoretical.
4. Individuals could be changed in practically any way one might wish if the environment could be appropriately controlled.
5. The strongest influence in shaping a person into the kind of person he becomes is his mother.

In general, the results supported Runkel's hypothesis; the students whose *I*-scales were incompatible with that of their instructor obtained lower grades. (For a more complete discussion of some of the subtleties of the study and of the results, see the original article.) The support was not strong. When it is realized how many factors militated against this hypothesis, however, the existence of any significant support at all is rather striking. First, a very large proportion of variance in grades is accounted for by aptitude, work habits, and interest in course material; none of these variables was controlled in Runkel's study. Second, it must be remembered that whereas it is possible to conclude that the *I*-scales of two individuals cannot be represented on the same *J*-scale, the conclusion that two *I*-scales are compatible does not at all imply that the individuals are viewing the stimuli on the same dimension; hence, the group of students whose *I*-scales are compatible with those of their instructor probably contained a rather large subgroup who in fact were viewing the stimuli on dimensions much different from that of their instructor. And finally, the fact that an individual's *I*-scale can be represented on a single dimension does not mean that the individual's preferences could not be determined by many dimensions.

6.4 An Example: Unfolding Detroit Women About Their Ideal Points

Family size is readily conceptualized as a single dimension consisting of number of children. Furthermore, it is natural to suppose that women have some concept of the number of children they want in their families, and that their preference for having various numbers of children is a function of how close these family sizes are to their ideal family size. Finally, it is reasonable to hypothesize that both the number of children desired and the relative distances between number of children on the dimension will vary as a function of the number of children already in the family.

These considerations led Goldberg and Coombs (1962) to apply the unfolding technique to women's preferences for number of children. That is, they assumed that these numbers could be represented by points on a single dimension and that a woman's I-scale indicating her preference for various numbers of children could also be represented by a point on the same dimension (in such a way that the rank order of the numbers from this point corresponded to the I-scale). Since the unfolding technique yields certain information about relative distances, Goldberg and Coombs used it to evaluate (p. 106) "the subjective distances between various numbers of children in the family." They were interested both in determining these distances for the entire sample as a means of evaluating "the present fertility norms" (p. 107), and in determining how these distances varied as a function of the number of children the women had already had.

The women sampled were from the "Detroit area study" (p. 108). "The sample consisted of 1215 women who had recently been married, or had given birth to their first, second, or fourth child. Most of the analysis is confined to the 1148 women who were classified as 'probably fecund.' " The observations consisted of these women's rank-order preference for the number of children they wanted in their families.

The assumption was made that the rank order of the number of children (i.e., stimuli) on the J-scale corresponded to number of children. Since Goldberg and Coombs were only interested in numbers from zero to six, this assumption means that the rank order of the numbers on the J-scale was 0, 1, 2, 3, 4, 5, 6. Notice that if a particular woman had strong feelings about not having an only child, her least preferred number of children would be one, and consequently she could not be represented on this J-scale (for the least preferred stimulus must be one of the two at the extremes of the scale). Goldberg and Coombs bypassed the problem raised by such possible preferences by not allowing them; that is, the women were questioned in such a way that they could not express such a preference.

They were first asked how many children they would ideally like to have. They were then asked whether they would prefer having one more, or one less. If they said they would prefer having one more, they were asked whether they would prefer having two more or one less, and so on. The procedure was repeated until a preference for zero or six children was indicated, at which point the remaining preferences were filled in by the experimenter in accord with the assumption. For example, if a woman indicated that ideally she would like to have four children, she was then asked whether she would prefer five children or three; if she indicated she would prefer five, she was then asked whether she

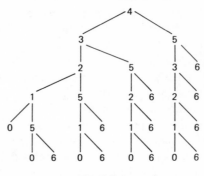

FIGURE 5.

would prefer six children or three; if she indicated she would prefer six, her I-scale was taken to be 4563210.

Figure 5 (from Goldberg & Coombs, p. 125) presents the branching procedure used to question a woman who said she would ideally like to have four children. Each time she indicated a preference, she was asked to choose between the two numbers directly below that preference; for example, if she indicated she would prefer three children to five, she was then asked whether she preferred two to five, and so on.

The results were analyzed separately for women who had had none, one, two, or four children. A technique devised by Goode was used to obtain a geometric representation of the relative distances implied by the unfolding technique.

Even though the women were not allowed to have rank orders inconsistent with the order zero to six on the J-scale, there were some inconsistencies in the

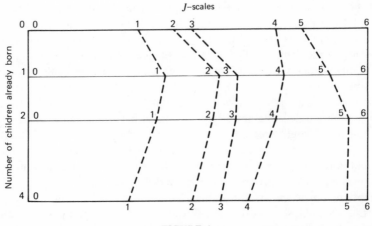

FIGURE 6.

data concerning the implications about relative distances. Goldberg and Coombs then constructed the J-scale so that the greatest number of I-scales could be represented on it; they termed such a J-scale a "dominant" one.

The results for the four groups of women are illustrated in Figure 6 (adapted from Goldberg & Coombs, p. 126). The figure presents each J-scale for each of the four groups; although the women within each group may differ in their preferences (I-scales), most are obtainable by folding the group J-scales about some point on it. It is of interest that for all women there is a large discrepancy between zero and one, and—somewhat surprisingly—the discrepancy between one and two remains constant irrespective of the number of children already in the family. Also of interest is the discrepancy between four and five, which becomes greater for the women with larger families; it is largest for the women who already have four children. Apparently, four children is an acceptable family size, but five is something of a brood.

6.5 Multidimensional Unfolding

The unfolding technique Coombs developed involves a *unidimensional* representation of people and stimuli. It can be naturally extended by not requiring that the representation be unidimensional, but instead by allowing people and stimuli to be represented in a *multidimensional* space—again according to the basic unfolding rule that stimulus j will be represented as closer to individual i than will stimulus k if and only if j is more psychologically proximal to i than is k. This extension was first proposed by Hays and Bennett (1961), and since that time several computer programs have been developed to achieve such a representation (e.g., McGee's, 1966; Gleason's, 1969).

Multidimensional unfolding techniques are basically nonmetric techniques that represent the conditional proximity of the stimuli to the people. In fact, there is only one crucial difference between the techniques devised to accomplish multidimensional unfolding and those devised to represent conditional proximity measures; the latter techniques (discussed in Section 4.3) represent stimuli where the conditional proximity of every stimulus to every other stimulus is observed; the unfolding techniques, in contrast, represent people and stimuli where only the conditional proximity of the stimuli to the people is observed; the conditional proximity of the people to the stimuli is not observed, that of the stimuli to each other is not observed, and that of the people to each other is not observed. Hence, a multidimensional unfolding technique is a nonmetric conditional proximity technique that works despite the fact most of the conditional proximity measures are unobserved. Figure 7 illustrates which conditional proximity measures are observed and which are not; notice that irrespective of the number of stimuli and people, there will always be more unobserved proximities than observed ones.

As was pointed out in Section 4.3, one of the basic problems with proximity techniques is that the consistency criteria are not well understood—and that

	People	Stimuli
People	Not observed	Observed
Stimuli	Not observed	Not observed

FIGURE 7.

those that are understood are difficult to violate. Multidimensional unfolding techniques have the same problem. In fact, the problem is exacerbated because the number of conditional proximity measures observed relative to the number of points is smaller in multidimensional unfolding than in multidimensional proximity analysis; furthermore, there are no constraints of the type illustrated in Figure 4 of Chapter IV because there is no evaluation of the relative distance of ideals from stimuli—only of the relative distance of stimuli from ideals.

Gleason (1969) has applied his multidimensional unfolding technique to sociometric observations. These observations were collected by Newcomb (1961); two groups of students living together in dorms rank ordered how much they liked their fellow dorm members each week for 17 weeks. Such sociometric observations are usually analyzed by a proximity technique. Each person is represented by a single point, and his stated preference for other people is represented by the distance between his point and the points representing them (the less the preference, the greater the distance). What Gleason did was to suggest that the point representing the individual's preference ranking should not necessarily be the same point that represents him as someone chosen by other people. For example, an unpopular isolate may well indicate a preference for the most popular people in the group, although they do not reciprocate his preferences; hence, the symmetry demanded by the usual proximity techniques may be violated. Moreover, when an individual is stating his preference for other individuals, he is conveying information about what people he likes—not about who likes him (although friendships in such a setting *tend* to be reciprocal). These considerations led Gleason to represent Newcomb's data with a multidimensional unfolding (computer program) technique that he developed. The representation satisfied the unfolding rule that the point representing an individual j is closer to the point representing individual i's ideal than is the point representing individual k if and only if i prefers j to k; i's preference of j to k or vice versa does not have any effect on the point representing individual i—only on the point representing his ideal; instead, the location of the point representing individual *i* is determined by the preference of *other people* for *him*.

One particularly intriguing aspect of Gleason's study is that once the spatial representation is obtained, it is possible to assess the distance between each individual *i* and his ideal point—and hence (indirectly) how much he would like himself. Unfortunately, this distance was not related to any of the other variables Gleason examined. (It should be noted, however, that Newcomb's original project was not concerned with this distance—and hence the variables he examined were not chosen to be related to it; other variables—for example, subjective measures of self-esteem—might well be.) Furthermore, Gleason cautions against a naive interpretation of this distance (1969, p. 118).

"Since there is no necessary reason why the attributes one prefers for himself should be the same as those most preferred in other people, it seems that caution should be exercised whenever interpreting the intrapersonal separation as a measure of self-esteem. The conditions under which a person's ideal self and his ideal friend are alike or discrepant might provide a fruitful area for further investigation."

QUESTIONS

1. The extended quote from Likert presented at the beginning of this chapter reads "Each statement should be of such a nature that persons with different points of view, so far as a particular attitude is concerned, will respond to it differently. Any statement to which persons with markedly different attitudes can respond in the same way is, of course, unsatisfactory." Show that the second sentence is logically equivalent to the first. (*Hint:* the first may be paraphrased as "for appropriate statements, different viewpoints imply different responses.")

2. Paraphrase the Likert quote interchanging the role of attitudes and statements.

3. In the text it was stated that the *I*-scales *ABCDE* and *CEDAB* are incompatible in that they could not both be represented by two points on the same *J*-scale. Demonstrate this assertion.

4. Although each pair of the following three *I*-scales could be represented on a common *J*-scale, all three taken together cannot. Show how each pair can be so represented and explain why all three cannot.

    ABCD
    DCBA
    DBAC

5. Following is a set of eleven *I*-scales. Using the technique developed in Section 6.2, unfold these onto a common *J*-scale.

1. *BCADE*
2. *CEBAD*
3. *DABCE*
4. *BADCE*
5. *ABDCE*
6. *ECBAD*
7. *CBADE*
8. *CBEAD*
9. *CBAED*
10. *BACDE*
11. *ADBCE*

Construct a dimension containing the relative distances implied by the order of the midpoints.

6. Suppose that Goldberg and Coombs had collected similarity judgments about family size instead of preferential choices. Is there any necessary connection between a spatial representation based on a proximity analysis of such judgments and the representation that Goldberg and Coombs actually obtained? How might discrepancies be interpreted?

7. It was stated in the text that constraints of the type illustrated in Figure 4 of Chapter IV do not occur in multidimensional unfolding. Explain why not.

8. The technique for jointly representing stimuli and people presented in the beginning of this chapter (see Figure 1) has been termed *parallelogram analysis* (Coombs, 1964, pp. 65-79). Develop a mechanism for performing a parallelogram analysis similar to that presented in Section 5.1 for obtaining a Guttman scale.

9. Techniques based on confusion were discussed in Chapters III and IV. Consider, now, the degree to which stimulus j is confused with stimulus k. Show how such confusions could be analyzed by unfolding techniques instead of by proximity techniques. Think of examples where unfolding techniques would be more appropriate; where proximity techniques would be more appropriate.

VII

Representational Measurement: General Issues

7.1 Coombs' Classification System

A man expresses an attitude toward a cigarette: "I like it." This statement may either be regarded as conveying information about the cigarette (it is like a breath of springtime), about the man (he is a virile individual), or about the interaction between the cigarette and the man (the harshness of the cigarette matches his desired level of harshness).

In the course of a public opinion survey, a man is asked whether he thinks all American troops should be withdrawn from Southeast Asia and he answers "yes." His answer may be regarded either as conveying information about a policy of withdrawal (it would be popular), or about him (he's in favor of withdrawal), or about the interaction between him and the policy (it is close enough to his ideal position that he endorses it).

And, in general, whenever an individual responds to a stimulus, his response may be viewed as conveying information about the stimulus, about him, or about the relationship between him and the stimulus. When such a response serves as a basis for representational measurement, the property being measured may either be a property of the individual, of the stimulus, or of the relationship between the individual and the stimulus.

Techniques that are used to measure properties of a stimulus are generally termed *psychophysical,* whereas those used to measure a property of the individual responding to the stimulus are generally termed *psychometric.* As C. I. Mosier (1940) pointed out years ago, however, all psychophysical measurement techniques can be applied *mutatis mutandis* to measuring properties of people, and all psychometric techniques can similarly be applied to measuring properties of stimuli. This possibility occurs because an individual's response to a stimulus can be regarded as providing information about either the individual or the stimulus; either the set of stimuli or of people can be used as standards to evaluate the other set. Any technique that uses people as standards to measure properties of stimuli (i.e., any psychophysical technique) can be applied to a

75

situation in which stimuli are used as standards to measure properties of people (i.e., a psychometric situation). And vice versa. Magnitude and proximity techniques are designed to measure properties of either people or stimuli alone.

In contrast, there are the interlocking and unfolding techniques that are designed to measure properties of people and stimuli jointly. If, for example, an investigator is interested in measuring the harshness of cigarettes and people's preference for harshness at the same time, he may ask people whether a given cigarette is too mild or too harsh; if the individual says that the cigarette is too harsh, the investigator may wish to represent the individual's ideal below the cigarette on the scale of harshness, but if the individual says the cigarette is too mild, the investigator may wish to represent the individual's ideal above the cigarette on that scale. That is, the investigator may wish to construct a Guttman scale of harshness.

Coombs (1964) has proposed that the distinction between measuring stimuli or people alone on the one hand and measuring the relationship between people and stimuli on the other may be generalized to a distinction between measuring *single* sets of entities and *multiple* sets of entities. For example, the Bogardus social distance scale—an interlocking technique—measures the relationship between social exclusion criteria and ethnic groups; even though both criteria and groups may exist "within the head" of a single individual, we represent both sets of entities on a social distance scale when that individual tells us, for example, that he would exclude Turks from living in his neighborhood. (Of course, there is nothing to prevent us from constructing a *group* distance scale by collapsing across a number of individuals.) The point is that representational measurement techniques may either reflect relationships between a single set of entities or between two or more distinct sets of entities.

The distinction between one-set techniques and multiset techniques is a basic dichotomy in Coombs' (1964) system of classification of representational measurement techniques. A second basic dichotomy that gives rise to this classification system may best be understood by examining the measurement scale for weight.

This scale has two fundamental properties: order and proximity. That is, the numbers that are assigned to objects and termed their weights are ordered (of any two unequal numbers, one is larger than the other), and the proximity of the numbers can also be assessed (the proximity of any two numbers is the absolute difference between them). Many other physical measurement scales have both these properties. It is possible, however, to find scales that have only one or another of these properties. For example, the Mohs' scale for measuring the hardness of objects only has the property of order (representing the fact that certain objects will scratch other objects), but no property of proximity (the difference between the hardness of two objects is not represented). For an example of measurement involving proximity but no order, consider the biological classification of species; two species are most similar if they belong to the same genus, least if they belong to different phyla.

Table 1   **The Coombs' Classification System**

	Basic property of scale	
	Order	Proximity
One-set	1. Magnitude techniques	2. Proximity technique
Multiset	3. Interlocking techniques	4. Unfolding techniques

Most measurement scales have at least one of these two properties. Since such a property of the measurement scale represents a crucial property of the thing being measured, measurement techniques may be dichotomized on the basis of whether this crucial property is represented by an *ordinal* relationship on the measurement scale or by a *proximity* relation. This dichotomy, considered jointly with the earlier dichotomy, leads to a fourfold classification of measurement techniques, which served as the basis for classifying techniques in Chapters III to VI. This system was first explicitly stated by Coombs (1964) and is illustrated in Table 1. Since *all* representational measurement techniques must represent either one set of entities or more than one set and since all must involve order or proximity or both, the classification system is exhaustive.

It should be pointed out that the above description of Coombs' system does not do it justice, but instead is oriented toward an elementary understanding of its most basic points. For example, a third dichotomy is included in the system as presented in its entirety (see Coombs, 1964). Also, a distinction is made between proximity per se and order relations between proximities; finally, the distinction between order and proximity is not given the primary importance that it is given in this book.

7.2 Observations Versus Data

A number of investigators concerned with population growth in the United States have observed that couples desiring children prefer to have at least one child of each sex. This preference is indicated by couples' stated preferences among various types of families (Freedman, Freedman, & Whelpton, 1960); it is also indicated by actual performance (Bumpass & Westoff, 1970; Dawes, 1970) in that women who have at least one child of each sex are less likely to have an additional child than are those who have all boys or all girls.

Consider, now, an investigator who observes couples' preferences among various family compositions (e.g., two girls versus two girls and a boy). Such preferences may be verbally stated or they may be inferred from couples' actual decisions about whether to have an additional child. How should such preferences be analyzed if the investigator is to represent his couples' attitudes toward family compositions?

He could analyze his observations by the Thurstone comparative judgment technique presented in Chapter II. The proportion of times that family composition *a* is preferred to family composition *b* in the investigator's sample could be used to estimate the probability with which *a* is preferred to *b* in the population from which the sample was drawn; then the various family compositions could be located on a dimension of preferability.

Or he could analyze his observations by the unfolding technique presented in Chapter VI. The rank order of each couple's preferences for various family compositions could be represented by the relative distances between these compositions and an ideal point corresponding to that couple's most preferred family.

Which analysis is *correct?* Both. If the investigator is interested in assessing the prevalence of present or future family compositions, he might accomplish his purpose better if he uses the Thurstone technique. If, however, he is interested in assessing the effect of sex control of children (see Markle & Nam, 1971) or the potential of various propaganda techniques, he might better analyze his observations using an unfolding technique; for example, he might discover that the family composition two boys-two girls is represented near the composition one boy-one girl in his resulting preference space, a result that could lead him to advocate concentration of propaganda efforts to persuade people with a boy and a girl not to have additional children—since people who want two boys and two girls might be almost as well satisfied by having a single boy and a single girl.[1]

Thus, the *observations themselves* do not determine the way in which they should be analyzed. This conclusion is emphasized by Coombs (1964), who distinguishes between observations and *"data."* Coombs maintains that an investigator has data only when he decides whether his observations shall be analyzed by a magnitude, proximity, interlocking, or unfolding method; that is, the investigator plays a "creative" role in determining the essential nature of the empirical representational system he is observing—a determination equivalent to deciding which type of technique is to be used to represent the observations. (Of course, it is often possible to use more than one type of technique to represent a given set of observations and then to compare the internal consistency of these types; as of the writing of this book, however, the author is aware of no generally accepted criteria for making such a comparison.)

---

[1] Interestingly, such preferences for sexual composition will affect family size, but *not* affect the ratio of males to females in the resulting population (Benjamin Winter, personal communication). The principle is simple. Preferences for sexual composition may affect the decision of whether to have an additional child, but people (presently) have no control over the sex of the children they have already had, and they have no control over the sex of a subsequent child if they decide to have one; hence, they have no control whatsoever, with the result that the sex ratio will be the same as it would have been if people had no such preferences. A preference for various sexual compositions will, however, have an effect on the *size* of families—because it will affect the decision of whether to have additional children.

Coombs' distinction between observations and data also helps to clarify the distinction between representational measurement and index measurement. Lack of consistency between observation and representation in representational measurement is regarded as "error" between observation and data; the probabilistic relationship between observation and indices in index measurement is regarded as intrinsic to the phenomena being indexed.

7.3 Scale Types

Weight can be measured in pounds, ounces, or grams—height in feet, inches, or centimeters. The prestige of occupations (Figure 3, Chapter III) can be measured in terms of any arbitrary units that represent the ratio or interval estimates of the subjects judging prestige, and a *J*-scale may be drawn in any way that illustrates the relative distances implied by the midpoint order. All these measurement scales may, then, be transformed in some way (e.g., multiplying number of pounds by 16 to obtain the number of ounces). The way in which a scale may be transformed defines the *type* of scale it is. Some scales (e.g., weight) may be transformed only by multiplying or dividing by a constant, although others (e.g., Guttman scales) may be stretched or contracted like rubber bands.

The principle for determining how a measurement scale may be transformed (Adams, Fagot, & Robinson, 1965) is really quite simple: a scale may be transformed in any way that does not change any implications about the empirical system it represents; it may not be transformed in such a way that these implications are changed. For example, an object weighing 5 pounds must perfectly balance an object weighing 3 pounds and an object weighing 2 pounds in a pan balance; this implication follows from the numerical fact that $5 = 3 + 2$. If the scale of weight is transformed by multiplying the weight of all objects by 7½, this implication is unchanged because the first object would now weigh 37.5 units, the second would weigh 22.5 units, and the third would weigh 15 units. If, however, the scale were transformed by adding 10 to the number of pounds, the implication would be changed because the first object would now be said to weigh 15 units, the second 13 units, and the third 12—which would imply that the first should no longer balance the other two. Transformations that do not affect the empirical implication are termed *permissible transformations,* and those that do are not permissible transformations.

The type of transformation that is permissible defines the *scale type* of the measurement procedure. To quote Stevens (1968, p. 850):

"The permissible transformations defining a scale type are those that keep intact the empirical information depicted by the scale. If the empirical information has been preserved, the scale form is said to remain invariant. The critical isomorphism [homeomorphism] is maintained."

Ratio Scales

Weight is a ratio scale. If all the weights in a particular set are transformed by multiplying them by a constant greater than zero, the implications about which would balance or outweigh which in a pan balance are unchanged; hence, multiplication by a constant is a permissible transformation. And, in fact, it is the only permissible transformation. Measurement scales in which multiplication by a constant is the only permissible transformation are termed *ratio* scales; the term comes from the fact that if two numbers are multiplied by a constant, the ratio between them remains unaltered.

The only examples of ratio scales discussed in this book are those in Chapter III that are meant to represent ratio judgments. Ratio scales are not very common in the domain of attitude measurement, since most of the implications about the empirical relations such measurement is meant to represent are unchanged by transformations more drastic than multiplication by a constant.

Interval Scales

Temperature is an interval scale. Equal intervals of temperature correspond to equal volumes of expansion of mercury. These intervals may, however, be measured either in terms of Fahrenheit or centigrade units. The temperature in Fahrenheit units equals 9/5 times the temperature in centigrade units plus 32. This relationship is of the form: $x' = ax + b$ $(a > 0)$. (In the example, x' is temperature in Fahrenheit, x is temperature in centigrade, a is 9/5, and b is 32.) Transformations of the form $x' = ax + b$ are termed *linear* because the graph of such a relationship between x' and x is a straight line.[2] Whenever such linear transformations are the only permissible transformation, the scale is termed an *interval* scale. Notice that multiplication by a constant may be accomplished by the linear transformation in which $b = 0$; hence, the type of permissible transformation that defines the ratio scale is also permissible on interval scales, but not vice versa.

The term "interval" scale derives from the fact that linear transformations leave the ratio of intervals unaffected. Consider, for example, the ratio of intervals $(x_1 - x_2)/(x_3 - x_4)$. If a linear tranformation of the form $x' = ax + b$ is applied to this ratio, the result is $((ax_1 - b) - (ax_2 - b))/((ax_3 - b) - (ax_4 - b))$, which equals $(ax_1 - ax_2)/(ax_3 - ax_4)$ because the b's cancel out—which equals $(x_1 - x_2)/(x_3 - x_4)$ because the a's cancel out.

An example of an interval scale discussed in this book was that of seriousness of crimes in Chapter II. The scale represents a probability that one crime is judged to be more serious than another; if a constant is added to the value of each crime, this probability is unaltered; if the value is multiplied by a constant, the probability is unaltered (provided, of course, that the deviations of the

---

[2] The term 'linear' enjoys wide use among psychologists; many mathematicians refer to such transformations as *'affine'* and reserve the term 'linear' for transformations here termed 'ratio'—i.e., transformations of the form $x' = ax$.

distributions are multiplied by the same constant); a linear transformation, which combines the previous two transformations, therefore leaves this probability unaltered.

Ordinal Scales

The Mohs' scale of hardness is an ordinal scale. (One mineral is ordered above another on this scale if and only if the first scratches the second but not vice versa; moreover, observations indicate that scratching is transitive—if mineral *a* scratches mineral *b* and *b* scratches *c*, then *a* scratches *c;* thus the order of minerals on the scale leads to correct implications about which scratch which.)[3] If minerals are assigned numbers to indicate their positions on this scale, then any transformation that preserves the order of the numbers is permissible. The scales for which only such order preserving transformation is permissible are termed *ordinal* scales. (Order preserving transformations are often termed *monotone* transformations.) Notice that, just as the multiplication by a constant is a special type of linear transformation, the linear transformation is a special type of monotone transformation.

Guttman scales are ordinal scales. *If* numbers were assigned to people and stimuli on the basis of which dominate which, then any monotone transformation of these numbers would yield the same implications about domination. In actual practice, numbers are rarely assigned to people or stimuli and, instead, the order itself is presented; one reason for not bothering to assign numbers is that a monotone transformation of a set of numbers may yield quite different numbers—and hence it seems arbitrary to pick one set of numbers instead of another.

7.4 The Scale Type of Index Measures and Statistical Manipulations of Indices

To ask what scale type is obtained by a particular index measurement technique is to ask a nonsensical question. Scale type is defined in terms of permissible transformations, which in turn are defined in terms of leaving the implications in the empirical relational system invariant. If there are no such implications, then the concept of permissible transformations is irrelevant—and hence the concept of scale type is irrelevant.

Unfortunately, however, this nonsensical question is occasionally asked, and occasionally answered (nonsensically). For example, ranks are often considered to constitute an ordinal scale, even though there is no empirical transitivity corresponding to the ranks. (Tennis player *a* may beat *b,* who beats *c,* who in turn beats *a*—because of the specific strengths and weaknesses of the three

---

[3] Note again that we *observe* transitivity; it is not true by definition. Suppose, for example, (Benjamin Winter, personal communication) that instead of scratching we observed "putting a dent in someone's ego." Transitivity may fail; *a* may know how to dent *b* and *b* may know how to dent *c,* but *c*'s defenses may make him immune to being dented by *a.*

players.) Once having decided such ranks *necessarily* form an ordinal scale, an investigator notes that monotone transformations on ranks are permissible and notes also that such transformations yield contradictory implications about average ranks. (Rank order four objects *a, b, c, d.* If the numbers 1, 2, 4, 7 are assigned, then the average of *a* and *d* (4) is larger than the average of *b* and *c* (3); if the numbers 1, 4, 6, 7 are assigned, then the average of *a* and *d* (4) is smaller than the average of *b* and *c* (5).) The investigator concludes with the maxim "you can't average rank orders." *Of course,* rank orders can be averaged; they are averaged almost daily in athletic competitions consisting of many individual events. The only point is that such average ranks do not necessarily have any empirical meaning other than that determined by *fiat* (e.g., swimming team *a* beats swimming team *b*).

Occasionally, index measures are regarded as representational because of the belief that only representational measures can be subjected to certain statistical manipulations. This belief is mistaken. As Hays writes (1963, p. 74) "If the statistical method involves the procedures of arithmetic used on numerical scores [however obtained] then the numerical answer is formally correct." Moreover, assumptions involved in statistical inference are assumptions about distributions of *numbers,* not about any real world phenomenon these numbers may or may not represent or index.

It is, however, true that if different indexing procedures are used, different statistical conclusions may follow (e.g., an experimenter may have a "significant" effect if he analyzes log latencies and an "insignificant" effect if he analyzes raw latencies—or if he assigns numbers to rating scale responses on one basis rather than on another). Representational measures, in contrast, often lead to invariant statistical conclusions under all permissible transformations; for example, the *t* value testing the difference between two sets of numbers will not change if all the numbers are subjected to a linear transformation. This invariance of statistical conclusion has led some investigators to assert that statistics *should* only be applied in a situation in which such invariance is assured by representational measures. The conclusion is a non sequitur.

Thus, Anderson (1961, p. 309) writes

". . . the statistical test can hardly be cognizant of the empirical meaning of the numbers with which it deals. Consequently the validity of the statistical inference cannot depend on the type [or nontype] of measurement scale used."

Stevens (1968, p. 849) responds to this "sequitur" by writing that

". . . however much we may agree that the statistical test cannot be cognizant of the empirical meaning of the numbers, the same privilege of ignorance can scarcely be extended to experimenters."

Or, as Hays succinctly states (1963, p. 74), "if nonsense is put into the mathematical system, nonsense is sure to come out." The point is that if numbers are to be manipulated to some purpose, they must have some empirical meaning, either as representational measures or as valid indices of something.

On rare occasion, an investigator will argue that *because* index measures can be statistically manipulated in productive ways, they are "really" representational measures. For example, Jensen uses this rationale for the assertion that IQ scores form an interval scale (1969, p. 23):

"In brief, IQs behave just about as much like an interval scale as do measurements of height, which we know for sure is an interval scale. [sic, height is a ratio scale.] Therefore, it is not unreasonable to treat the IQ as an interval scale."

IQs are very useful numbers, but they do not lie on an interval scale—because there is no empirical relation system that they represent. The performance of someone on an IQ test determines the IQ number assigned to him, but these numbers do not yield any implications about some empirical relation (other than the trivial information about how the person scored on the IQ test).

Multiplication by a constant does not affect ratios of numbers, nor ratios of differences between numbers—nor does it affect the order of numbers. A linear transformation (where $b \neq 0$) does affect the ratio of the numbers, but it does not affect the ratio of distances, nor the order; a monotone transformation that is not linear affects both the ratios and the ratios of the differences, but again not the orders. Hence, the idea seems to have arisen that the ratio scale is somehow better than an interval scale, which in turn is somehow better than an ordinal scale—which in turn leads to the idea that a psychologist somehow *should* attempt to measure important properties on ratio scales. As has been pointed out throughout this book, however, the question of how something may be measured is an empirical one—and as pointed out in this chapter, the question of the scale type is dependent on the behavior of the empirical relational system. Furthermore, the value of measurement does not primarily lie in the type of scale obtained (nor in the scale values) but in the discovery and explication of the lawfulness inherent in the phenomenon that *permits* measurement to occur.

7.5 Fundamental Measurement

In previous chapters, it has been emphasized that certain consistency conditions must be satisfied if a given measurement technique is to be successful. That is, *if* the numerical representation is to be consistent, *then* certain observations must be made and other observations must not. This inference is illustrated in Figure 1*a*.

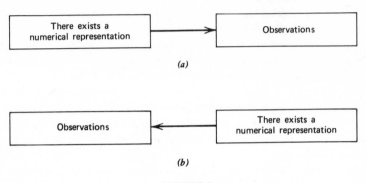

FIGURE 1.

In some situations, it is possible to make the *inverse* inference, that is, *if* certain observations are made and others are not, *then* it is possible to construct a numerical representation. This inference is illustrated in Figure 1*b*. When it is possible to make such an inference, the applicability of a measurement technique may be established by noting whether the empirical observations implying its existence are in fact observed. Such establishment is termed *fundamental* measurement—in the sense that it is based purely on observation instead of on some assignment of number or order to the entities being measured. Moreover, the observations are always of an *ordinal* nature.

The first theory of fundamental measurement was developed by Hölder (1901), who was concerned with the measurement of weight. He showed that *if* the behavior of objects in a pan balance satisfied certain conditions (often termed "axioms"), *then* numbers (i.e., weights) could be assigned to these objects to represent their behavior, and any two sets of numbers so assigned must be proportional to each other—that is, weight is a ratio scale. The basic conditions (axioms) were all of an ordinal nature. Examples of such conditions follow:

Transitivity: if *a* outweighs *b* and *b* outweighs *c,* then *a* must outweigh *c.*

Cancellation: a outweighs *b* if and only if *a* and *c* outweigh *b* and *c.*

Positivity: the combination of *a* with *b* outweighs both *a* and *b* alone.

Density: if *a* outweighs *b,* then there exists some object *a'* that *a* outweighs and that in turn outweighs *b.*

It is clear that if all positive numbers are to represent weights, then these conditions must be satisfied; numbers are transitive, the addition or subtraction of a number from an inequality preserves that inequality, the sum of two positive numbers is always greater than either, and there is always a number between any two distinct other numbers. Hölder proved that if certain similar conditions are satisfied, then numerical weights can be assigned in a consistent manner, and these weights form a ratio scale. (See Figure 1*b*)[4]

In general, *measurement techniques of the type discussed in Chapters III to VI are applicable if and only if certain empirical conditions are satisfied. Some of these conditions are those used in the evaluation of the consistency of the measurement technique; others are what are termed "technical" conditions. The particular conditions that must be satisfied vary from technique to technique.* For example, the density condition specified above is a "technical" one—in that it would not be used to check the *consistency* of the numerical weights assigned to objects. (That is, if we cannot find an object whose weight falls between that of two others, we cannot conclude that the weights already assigned are *inconsistent* but, instead, that such an object does not exist or that we have simply failed to find it.)

It follows that the consistency conditions are necessary for measurement to occur. And, indeed, these consistency conditions were shown to be necessary. What was not discussed in the previous chapters was that these conditions together with some others (the technical ones) insure the existence of the numerical representation termed "measurement" (see Figure 1). In fact, while most of these consistency conditions may have seemed "intuitively obvious," many of them were chosen just because they, in conjunction with the technical conditions, assured the existence of a measurement scale.

It would be nice to be able to specify the other (technical) conditions that must be met in each measurement context and to state exactly which consistency checks in conjunction with these other conditions guaranteed the existence of a measurement scale. Unfortunately, however, these conditions must be specified separately for each measurement technique, and they have not (yet) been specified for many of the measurement techniques discussed in this book; furthermore, the technical conditions are often not applicable to the attitude measurement domain—in which the investigators are almost always dealing with finite sets of stimuli and people. (The interested—and mathematically sophisticated—reader is referred to Luce and Tukey (1964) for a discussion of these conditions in the context of "conjoint measurement," or to Tversky (1967) for a discussion of these conditions in one particular finite context.)

Since it is possible for many measurement techniques to find a set of conditions that form a *sufficient* condition for the measurement technique to be applied, it is possible to check these conditions empirically; if the conditions are satisfied, then the measurement technique is known to be applicable; if one or more of them are not satisfied, the measurement technique cannot be applied—

---

[4] In fact, it can be proved that the above four conditions—together with two others—imply the existence of a ratio scale of weight (Suppes & Zinnes, 1963). For an extended discussion of Hölder's original work and its generalization, see Chapter 2 of Krantz, Luce, Suppes, & Tversky (1971).

since each of them considered singly is a *necessary* condition for the application of the technique. Fundamental measurement involves the evaluation of these conditions. As was pointed out at the beginning of this section, the conditions need not be evaluated by actually assigning numbers to the entities to be measured, but may be evaluated on the basis of purely qualitative aspects of one's observations.

Although this fundamental measurement approach has not yet been used in the domain of attitude measurement, it has been used in other contexts in psychology in which measurement has been desired. (See the above references.) It is, then, possible that in the future fundamental measurement will play a role in attitude measurement. At the present, it is not possible to predict how large this role will be.

7.6 Functional Measurement

Anderson (1970) has coined the term *functional measurement* to describe a type of measurement that is slightly different from that described in the previous chapters. It is similar to representational measurement in that it requires consistency between observation and numerical representation. It is different in that *the consistency tests for functional measurement rely not only on properties of the numerical representation but on these properties considered in conjunction with a theory.* For example, Anderson has proposed a theory about how people combine evaluative information about other individuals in order to arrive at an overall evaluative attitude—specifically, his theory predicts how the ratings of other individuals based on single adjectives describing these individuals will be related to ratings based on sets of these adjectives. (For example, his theory predicts how the ratings of an individual described only as "sincere" and one described only as "pleasant" will be related to the ratings of an individual described as both sincere and pleasant.) What the theory consists of is a formula that predicts such ratings on a scale centered about zero; the numbers assigned to individuals described by these adjectives provide information about certain elements of this formula, and then this information *taken together with the formula* leads to conclusions about further ratings.

Before describing Anderson's evaluative rating model in detail, a much simpler model will be proposed for didactic purposes—a model that turns out to be incorrect. Consider a set of adjectives $(a_1, a_2, \ldots, a_n)$ each of which has an evaluative rating $(A_1, A_2, \ldots, A_n)$; consider also, that the theory of impression formation states that the evaluative rating a person makes of an individual who is described by any subset $(a_1, a_2, \ldots, a_m)$ of these adjectives is given by the formula

$$\frac{1}{m}(A_1 + A_2 + \ldots + A_m) \, ,$$

that is, the overall rating is simply the average of the component ratings.

It follows that if the adjective "sincere" is given a rating of +3 and the adjective "pleasant" is given a rating of +2, then a person who is described as both sincere and pleasant should be given a rating of +2.5. There is nothing in the measurement scale itself that demands that a person described as sincere and pleasant must be given a rating of +2.5; the fact that sincere is given a rating of 3 and pleasant a rating of 2 implies that the combination should be given a rating of 2.5 only according to the theory that such ratings are averaged. Hence, it is the numbers together with the theory about how people form impressions that leads to the constraints on potential observations, not just the numbers together with the rules of arithmetic.

As was mentioned above, this theory is not valid—or at least not supported by data collected by Anderson and others interested in the problem of how people form evaluative attitudes. (See Fishbein & Hunter, 1964; Manis, Gleason, & Dawes, 1966; or the long list of Anderson's studies referenced in Anderson, 1970.) The problem with this model is that two adjectives given the same rating when combined will produce a rating that is more polarized (i.e., more positive if both ratings are positive, or more negative if both are negative). This observation clearly contradicts the simple averaging model proposed above. To account for this observation, Anderson proposed that people rating other people are always integrating the information supplied by the adjectives with an initial impression; thus, two adjectives with the same evaluative connotation would move this initial impression farther than would either of these adjectives singly. Anderson proposes the following formulation

$$\text{Rating}, R = \frac{wk\bar{A} + (1 - w)I_0}{wk + (1 - w)} ,$$

where k is the number of adjectives and adjective set, $\bar{A}$ is the average value of the adjectives, I_0 is the initial impression, and w is the relative weighting given to the adjectives as opposed to the initial impression. Notice that $\bar{A}$ does not correspond to the average of the ratings of each adjective considered singly because those ratings involve the integration of the information given by the adjective with the initial impression. (That is, when there is only one adjective a_i, in the set and hence $\bar{A} = A_i$, the rating for a_i is not equal to A_i but is instead equal to $wA_i + (1-w)I_0$.)

In most of his work with this theory, Anderson assumes that $I_0 = 0$, in which case the formula becomes

$$R = \frac{wk\bar{A}}{wk + (1 - w)} .$$

Suppose, for example, that an individual rates someone described as sincere as +3 (i.e., $R = +3$), someone described as pleasant as +2, and someone described as clever as +2. Since these are single adjectives, $k = 1$ in the formula, and it follows that the value (A) assigned to sincere (S) is equal to $3/w$, to pleasant (P) is equal to $2/w$, and to clever (C) is equal to $2/w$. Then, the rating that should be assigned to someone described as both sincere and pleasant is $5/(1 + w)$. $((S + P)/2 = 5/2w$, hence $wk\bar{A}$ for the set S and P equals w times 2 times $5/2w$, or 5; $wk + (1 - w)$ for the set S and P equals $2w + 1 - w = 1 + w$.) The rating for someone described as both sincere and clever should be $5/(1 + w)$, and as both pleasant and clever should be $4/(1 + w)$. Notice that all these ratings involve w, which is unknown. The consistency of the theory is evaluated by determining whether the value for w estimated from all three ratings is consistent. This consistency check is illustrated in Figure 2.

As illustrated in Figure 2, the theory is essential for evaluating the consistency with which subjects assign evaluative ratings to indicate their attitudes toward the people described by the adjective sets. Conversely, it may be argued that these ratings are an integral part of the theory. To quote Anderson (1967, p. 164):

"The main argument for response validity rests on the goodness-of-fit which in fact provides a joint test of the model and the scale of measurement. Indeed, the scale of measurement may in general be considered as an integral part of the theory."[5]

What Anderson has termed functional measurement is quite common in contexts in which investigators attempt to evaluate different theories of attitude formation. The theory, together with some numerical response generated by the subject, provides constraints—and the theory and responses' consistency are jointly evaluated by some "goodness-of-fit" procedure. As has been emphasized throughout this book, it is not always clear how bad the fit must be before the investigator decides his observations fail the "goodness-of-fit" test; the situation in evaluating what Anderson has termed functional measurement is no different from that in evaluating the types of measurement discussed in earlier chapters.

One possible way to bypass this goodness-of-fit problem is to collect observations meant to distinguish between two or more theories (i.e., perform a "crucial experiment"). For example, a crucial test between Anderson's theory and the simple averaging theory first proposed is that Anderson's theory predicts that an individual described by two adjectives given the same evaluative rating will be rated as more polarized than will an individual described by either of these

---

[5] One controversy has arisen (Krantz & Tversky, 1971; Anderson, 1971) because Anderson also states that he is willing to make any monotone transformation on his rating scale output in order to achieve a good fit with his theory; thus, the resulting implications appear to be simply ordinal, as in fundamental measurement. In this author's opinion, much of this controversy has arisen over the ambiguity of the term "any." When Anderson uses the term, he is using it in the sense of the man who states that he will pay any price to preserve the health of his children. He is not indifferent between all possible bills; he would prefer small ones. That is, Anderson would like the numerical ratings to fit the theory as exactly as possible, but he is willing to perform some monotone transformation on them if they don't; in contrast, fundamental measurement is concerned *only* with the ordinal properties of the empirical system under investigation.

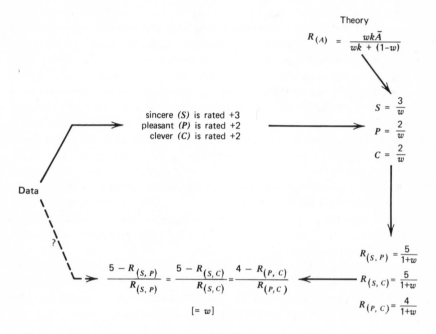

FIGURE 2.

adjectives taken alone, whereas the early model does not. It is then possible to reject the earlier model on the basis of the simple *qualitative* observation that individuals described by such pairs of adjectives are given more polarized ratings. And, in fact, it turns out that there are many such qualitative ways of distinguishing between different theories of impression formation (see Dawes-Saraga, 1968).

QUESTIONS

1. Virtually all advertisements show an individual enjoying a product. The advertiser does not, however, make the possible multiset interpretation that this particular individual enjoys this particular product but, instead, he makes what might be termed a "psychophysical pitch" (that the product is superior) or what might be termed a "psychometric pitch" (that the individual is superior). Observe a number of television commercials and see whether they can be classified as making a psychometric or psychophysical pitch. Which type of pitch do you think is better? (A student of mine, Paul Klinger, collected data on cigarette sales in 1964 that suggested that the psychometric pitch might be better.)

2. In what situations would it be most reasonable to analyze observations of the form individual i prefers stimulus j to stimulus k by using an unfolding technique, and in what situations would it be most appropriate to use a magnitude technique?

3. Thurstone developed a magnitude technique that he used to measure the judged seriousness of crimes. Could his observations, which were always of the form that individual i said crime j was more serious than crime k, be reasonably analyzed using different types of measurement techniques? That is, what would happen if these observations were given a multiset instead of a one-set interpretation or were interpreted in terms of proximity instead of order?

4. What sort of measurement scale is that representing distance? Time? Social distance? Proximity?

5. Let $x' = ax + b$ be a linear transformation of x. Plot x' as a function of x using standard Cartesian coordinates where x' is plotted on the ordinate and x on the abscissa. Interpret both a and b in terms of this plot.

6. A ratio scale is often said to be invariant under "expansion"; but an interval scale is said to be invariant under "expansion and displacement." Explain these characterizations.

7. Could it be argued that the measurement of weight is really functional measurement in Anderson's sense because we have a theory about what happens to objects when they are placed together in a pan balance (e.g., that no demon automatically adds or substracts some quantity of matter)?

Index Measurement

The representational measurement techniques presented in Section Two of this book all involve the establishment of a two-way relationship between an empirical relational system and a numerical one. Observations led to the construction of attitude scales and, in turn, these scales led to predictions about other observations. Thus, the measurement scales presented have the same basic status as does that of weight—in which numbers are assigned to objects on the basis of their observed behavior in a pan balance, and the numbers so assigned lead to predictions about future behavior in a pan balance.

In contrast, Section Three will deal with the type of technique that has been labeled *index measurement* in Chapter II. Such techniques are like standard measurement techniques in that measurement scales are systematically constructed on the basis of observation. Unlike standard measurement scales, however, these measurement scales do not constrain future observations. Instead, the justification for these scales is found in their utility. (Again, see Chapter II.) For example, a man may receive a numerical rating meant to indicate his attitude toward the President of the United States on the basis of a series of questions he answers; this number may be quite useful in predicting the man's behavior—how he will vote, whether he will write letters to the editor in opposition to his President, and so on. The number does not, however, constrain his answers to future questions about the President in the same sense that the weights assigned to objects constrain their future behavior in a pan balance.

It must again be emphasized (as it was in Chapter II) that the distinction between representational measurement and index measurement should not be interpreted as meaning that they are not alike in many ways. If the numerical rating we give a man to assess his attitude toward the President does not tell us *anything* about his future behavior vis-à-vis the President, it could hardly be useful. Thus, it places constraints. But the domain of the constraints is less well articulated than is the domain of the constraints placed by representational measurement techniques.

This section consists of three chapters: one describes rating scales, one discusses indirect assessment techniques, and one presents the evaluation of individual differences in attitudes as a function of differences in attitude statement endorsement. The organization of this section is more arbitrary than that of Section Two—which followed Coombs' classification scheme for representational measurement techniques. Nevertheless, an attempt is made to cover each of the major index measurement techniques in one or more of these chapters.

The Ubiquitous
Rating Scale

8.1 Introduction

Rating scale techniques are those that attempt to assess an individual's attitude by asking him to express that attitude in terms of a categorical or numerical rating. Thus, rating scales consist of categories (usually ordered), numbers, or lines. Sometimes they consist of combinations of categories, numbers, and lines. The individual whose attitude is being assessed is usually asked to select a single category, to select a single number, or to place a check mark on a single position on the line; sometimes he is asked to do something more complicated—for example, to indicate on a line a range of positions that he finds acceptable.

Five examples of rating scales are presented in Figure 1. Example 1*a* is taken from the work on *The Authoritarian Personality* by Adorno et al. (1950). The subject is presented with statements that express authoritarian attitudes, and he is to indicate his agreement with each statement by selecting a number from +3 to −3. Notice that he must select an integer value, and that verbal categories are paired with each such integer. Notice also that he cannot express complete indifference toward a statement; there is no 0 on the rating scale. (The first statement is taken directly from the original scale of authoritarianism; the second is an adaptation that is used more frequently than is the original from which it was adapted.)

The following statements refer to opinions regarding a number of social groups and issues, about which some people agree and others disagree. Please mark each statement in the left-hand margin according to your agreement or disagreement, as follows:

+1: slight support, agreement   −1: slight opposition, disagreement
+2: moderate support, agreement   −2: moderate opposition, disagreement
+3: strong support, agreement   −3: strong opposition, disagreement

Sciences like chemistry, physics, and medicine have carried men very far, but there are many important things that can never possibly be understood by the human mind.

Most people don't realize the extent to which their lives are governed by secret plots hatched in hidden places.

FIGURE 1. *(a)*

MY FATHER active−:−:−:−:−:−:−passive
MY FATHER soft−:−:−:−:−:−:−hard

(b)

Please rate program
by circling your choice.

       Excellent
       Very Good
       Good
       Poor

(c)

How attractive is this playmate?

0   20   40   60   80   100
Not at all   slightly   moderately   very   extremely

(d)

How much would you like to work at this job
in the army for the next two years?

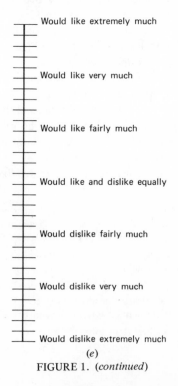

Would like extremely much

Would like very much

Would like fairly much

Would like and dislike equally

Would dislike fairly much

Would dislike very much

Would dislike extremely much

(e)

FIGURE 1. (continued)

94

Example 1*b* is that of the semantic rating scales used by Osgood and his associates (Osgood, Suci, & Tannenbaum, 1957). Here also the subject is to make a rating between two extreme positions; this rating is to indicate his feelings about the concept presented to the left of the scale. Here, the extremes of this scale are defined in terms of bipolar semantic adjectives instead of in terms of agreement or disagreement; furthermore, the positions between the extremes are not paired with verbal labels—although the midposition is clearly meant to be used when the rater associates the concept with neither pole of the adjective pair.

Example 1*c* is taken from a study by Sikes and Cleveland (1968) in which police and community members engaged in a program of face-to-face confrontation that was meant to alleviate tensions. After the program was over, each participant was asked to rate its success by choosing one of the four evaluative labels: excellent, very good, good, poor. Notice that although these labels are generally regarded as being on a continuum from poor to excellent, the individual responding is unable to indicate varying degrees of unfavorableness; yet he is able to indicate varying degrees of favorability.

Example 1*d* is taken from a study by Valins (1966), which attempted to manipulate male subjects' attitudes toward *Playboy* Playmate pictures by giving the subjects false information about their heart rates while they were looking at the pictures. Here, the subject is able to choose any number between 0 and 100 to indicate his feelings about attractiveness; he is not constrained to choose among only a few alternatives. Another important difference between this scale and previous scales is that the verbal categorizations are associated with a range of numerical values instead of with a single response.

The final example (1*e*) is taken from a study by Walster (Festinger et al., 1964, pp. 112–128) in which the attitude of inductees toward military jobs was assessed at varying times after they had chosen between two of them. This attitude scale is essentially like that presented in 1*d*, with the exception that the verbal labels are associated with single points on the scale, and that subjects may therefore make a response "between" two labels.

There are many types of rating scales in addition to those presented in Figure 1; they range from simple types that require a subject to respond only "yes" or "no" to those as complex as the one presented in Figure 1*e*. Rating scales are found throughout social psychology, especially in research concerned with people's attitudes. For example, almost all public opinion surveys use rating scales—in that the subject is asked to express his attitude directly by using a verbal category (e.g., he must choose the category "strongly approve," "approve," "disapprove," or "strongly disapprove" to express his attitude toward the President's handling of his job). Furthermore, a great deal of research on attitude change defines such change in terms of changes in rating scale behavior; for example, the 1964 book by Festinger et al. presents 10 studies in which experimenters investigated attitude change; in 7 of these 10 studies the subjects' attitudes were assessed by rating scale methods, and *only* by rating scale methods.

Rating scales are ubiquitous—in psychology, and in sociology and political science as well. For example, roughly 60 percent of the experimental articles published in the *Journal of Personality and Social Psychology* in 1970 used rating scale reponses as a dependent (i.e., manipulated) variable, and in approximately 60 percent of these, rating scale responses were the *only* dependent variables studied.[1]

The measurement methods discussed thus far in this book that are most like rating scale methods are those of ratio and interval estimation (Chapter III). The similarity lies in the fact that these methods, like rating scale methods, require the subject to make a direct subjective estimation of some property (e.g., to make a direct estimate of his feelings about occupational prestige). The crucial difference, however, lies in the fact that the ratio and interval estimation techniques contain consistency checks, whereas rating scale techniques do not. The individual who says that occupation a is twice as prestigious as is occupation b and that occupation b is twice as prestigious as is occupation c must then say that occupation a is four times as prestigious as is occupation c; in contrast, the individual who chooses the category "approve" to express his attitude toward his President is not constrained in his response to the next item on the pollster's questionnaire; he may be regarded as a bizarre individual if he then chooses "Communist" as a response to a question concerning political affiliation, but there is nothing *inconsistent* about his doing so. Perhaps he approves of the President's actions because he thinks that they play into the hands of the Communists.

8.2 The Semantic Differential

One of the most ubiquitous of all the rating scale techniques is the *semantic differential* (Osgood, Suci, & Tannenbaum, 1957). This "differential" consists of a set of bipolar semantic scales such as those illustrated in Figure 1*b;* these scales are anchored at each pole by an adjective describing one side of a semantic continuum. The subject is to rate a concept by placing his check mark at the point on this continuum where he feels that concept lies. Consider, for example, the subject asked to rate the concept FATHER on the active-passive scale, as in Figure 1*b*. If he thinks of his father as a very active person, he should place his mark in the most extreme category—that is, next to the word "active." If he thinks of him as only a slightly active person, he should place his check mark in the category just on the "active" side of the middle category; if he thinks of his

---

[1] The total number of experimental articles published was 172. Of these, 105 used rating scale responses as a dependent variable and in 61 of these there were no dependent variables other than such responses. These numbers are based on a survey performed by me, which was replicated independently by my secretary, Jan Thoele; we disagreed about the classification of only one study.

father as neither active nor passive, he should place his check mark in the middle category, and so on.

The purpose of the semantic differential is to assess the semantic connotations of the concept being rated. It is termed a "differential" because it is meant to show how concepts differ in these connotations to the individual rating them.

The three major types of scales used assess the semantic dimensions of evaluation (i.e., good-bad), potency (i.e., strong-weak), and activity (i.e., active-passive). The reason for concentrating on these three dimensions is that a number of factor analytic studies (see Chapter IV)—using people from 26 different cultures all around the world—have demonstrated them to be the most important factors of semantic connotation; that is, if we know how an individual rates a concept on these three factors, we can fairly well predict how he will rate it on a wide variety of bipolar semantic scales. And although these factors in the context of the factor analytic studies are *hypothetical* variables, they correspond very closely to the actual semantic scales defined by the adjectives "good-bad," "strong-weak," and "active-passive." Because this correspondence is not perfect and because the reliability of the single scales is low, additional scales (dimensions) are used to evaluate these three factors. Three or four scales are used to assess each; for example, the scales good-bad, tasty-distasteful, and valuable-worthless may be used to assess the evaluative dimension.

Usually, the location of the concept on each of the three dimensions is determined by averaging the ratings assigned to it on the three or four bipolar scales meant to evaluate that dimension; these averages are obtained by assigning values from 1 to 7 to correspond to each category on the scales. Once these values on each dimension are obtained, it is possible to represent the concept in a three-dimensional space and to evaluate the distance between concepts in that space. Osgood and Luria (1954, p. 580) believe that such distance represents "difference in meaning." They further propose that it is possible to study changes in meaning by observing changes in location in the space.

The semantic differential can be used in a variety of situations. It is, for example, possible to ask people of varying political persuasions to rate candidates for President (Kjeldahl, 1969). It is possible to ask people in a group or family situation to rate each other; it is even possible to construct a pure "projective" test by asking people to think up their own concepts and then rate them.

One particular strength of the technique is that it can be used *intra-individually;* that is, a semantic space can be constructed separately for each individual to represent the ways he views the concepts he rates; there is no need to collect observations from a number of people and then pool these observations in some way—as, for example, there was in the measurement of seriousness of crimes discussed in Chapter II. Since the technique can be used to assess intraindividual changes in attitude, it is useful in situations where an attempt is being made to change a single individual's attitude—in particular, in psychotherapy. Here, one of the problems of the person entering therapy is that he has an unhappy and personally stifling set of attitudes, particularly toward himself, and the success of the therapy can be determined *partly* by how these attitudes change. The patient must become less self-centered but simultaneously more accepting of himself and other important people in his life.

Osgood and Luria (1954) have engaged in an extensive investigation of psycho- therapeutic change as evidence by change in semantic differential ratings. The concepts that they asked patients to rate and the scales they used are presented in Table 1 (Osgood & Luria, 1954, p. 580). The coefficients in the bottom of this table are the "factor loadings"—which are the correlations between the scales actually used and the three hypothetical variables of evaluation, activity, and potency.

In 1953 the editor of the *Journal of Abnormal and Social Psychology*, Professor J. McV. Hunt, received a manuscript from Drs. Thigpen and Cleckley describing a case history of a woman with multiple personalities. This manuscript was later developed into a best-selling book titled *The Three Faces of Eve* (Thigpen & Cleckley, 1957), which in turn was adapted into a movie with the same title. (Joanne Woodward won the best actress award for her portrayal of the woman with the three personalities.) This movie is still shown periodically on television.

Hunt was aware of the work of Osgood and Luria when he received the Thigpen and Cleckley manuscript. He thought that it would be interesting to have semantic data from each of the "personalities" in the patient; thus, he

Table 1   Concepts And Scales Used in This Analysis

Concepts		
LOVE	MENTAL SICKNESS	SELF-CONTROL
CHILD	MY MOTHER	HATRED
MY DOCTOR	PEACE OF MIND	MY FATHER
ME	MIND	CONFUSION
MY JOB	FRAUD	SEX
	MY SPOUSE	

Scales and Their Factor Loadings			
Scales	Evaluation	Activity	Potency
valuable-worthless	.79	.13	.04
clean-dirty	.82	.03	−.05
tasty-distasteful	.77	−.11	.05
fast-slow	.01	.70	.00
active-passive	.14	.59	.04
hot-cold	−.04	.46	−.06
large-small	.06	.34	.62
strong-weak	.19	.20	.62
deep-shallow	.27	.14	.46
tense-relaxed	−.55	.37	−.12

contacted Thigpen and Cleckley to suggest that they administer the semantic differential, which they did—twice to each of the three personalities. Hunt also thought it would be "rather intriguing" to test the validity of the semantic differential by having Osgood and Luria attempt to describe each of the three personalities on the basis of the semantic differential data knowing little else about the patient. Osgood and Luria agreed, and they further agreed to publish the results of their blind analysis. In the ensuing publication, they described what they knew about the patient as follows:

"At this point we should state exactly what information we have about this case. We know that we are dealing with a case of triple personality, and these have been labeled for us (presumably by the therapists who collected the semantic data) 'Eve White,' 'Eve Black,' and 'Jane.' We suppose that the 'White' and 'Black' have some connotative significance—certainly, as will be seen, the quantitative semantic data distinguish sharply between them. We also know, of course, that the patient is a woman, presumably participating in some kind of therapy; we do not know the stage of therapy or whether or not she is hospitalized. We consider it also fair to ask (from J. McV. Hunt) about the following items of sociological status, because they contribute to the meaningful interpretation of certain concepts: Concept CHILD—does this woman have a child? Yes, she does. Concept SPOUSE—is this woman married? Yes, she is. Concepts FATHER and MOTHER—are her parents alive? The mother is, but Hunt doesn't know about the father. Concept MY JOB—has this woman had a job outside of homekeeping? Yes, she has. This is the sum total of our external information about the case.

"The semantic differential was given to this woman twice while 'in' each of her three personalities; a period of about 2 months intervened between the two testings."

The locations of the concept for Eve White at times 1 and 2 are presented in Figures 2 and 3. The evaluative dimension is represented vertically (with good up and bad down), the activity dimension is represented from left to right (with active left and passive right), and the potency dimension is represented by depth (with weak near to or toward the viewer and strong away from the viewer).

Osgood and Luria describe Eve White as follows (1954, pp. 581-582):

"The most general characterization would be that Eve White perceives "the world' in an essentially normal fashion, is well socialized, but has an unsatisfactory attitude toward herself. Here the usual societal 'goods' are seen favorably— MY DOCTOR, MY FATHER, LOVE, SELF-CONTROL, PEACE OF MIND, and MY MOTHER are all good and strong whereas FRAUD, HATRED, and to some extent CONFUSION are bad. The chief evidence of disturbance in the personality is the fact that ME (the self concept) is considered a little bad, a little passive, and definitely weak. Substantiating evidence is the weakness of her CHILD, as

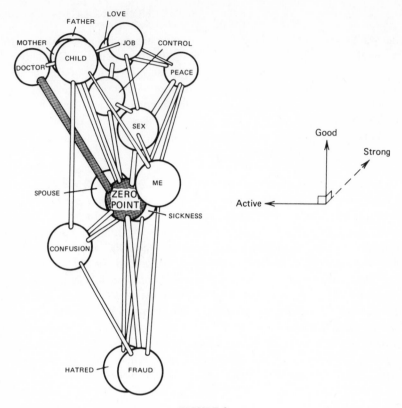

FIGURE 2.

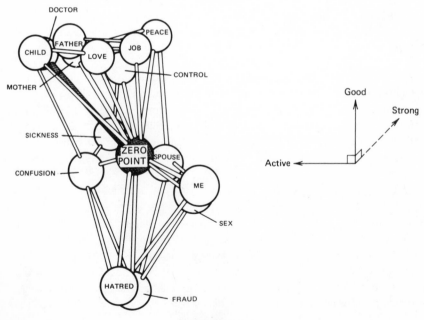

FIGURE 3.

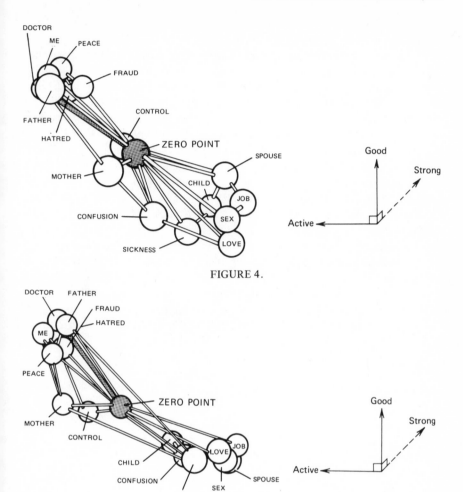

FIGURE 4.

FIGURE 5.

*she sees him (or her), and the essential meaninglessness to her of MY SPOUSE
and SEX. Note also the wide evaluative separation between LOVE and SEX. In
the interval between testings 1 and 2 ME and SEX become more bad and passive
and simultaneously become almost identical in meaning to her—and note that
her conceptions of LOVE (a good, strong thing) and SEX (a bad, weak thing like
herself) have moved still further apart."*

The locations of the concepts for Eve Black at times 1 and 2 are illustrated
in Figures 4 and 5. Again, the evaluative dimension is represented vertically
(with good up and bad down), the activity dimension is represented from left to
right (with active left and passive right), and the potency dimension is represented by depth (with weak near to or toward the viewer and strong away from
the viewer).

Osgood and Luria describe Eve Black as follows (1954, pp. 584-585):

"The most general characterization here would be that Eve Black has achieved a violent kind of adjustment in which she perceives herself as literally perfect, but, to accomplish this break, her way of perceiving 'the world' becomes completely disoriented from the norm. *The only exceptions to this dictum are MY DOCTOR and PEACE OF MIND, which maintain their* good *and* strong *characteristics, the latter, interestingly enough, also becoming* active *on 2. But if Eve Black perceives herself as being* good, *then she also has to accept HATRED and FRAUD as positive values, since (we assume) she has strong hatreds and is socially fraudulent. So we find a tight, but very un-normal, favorable cluster of ME, MY DOCTOR, PEACE OF MIND, HATRED, and FRAUD. What are positive values for most people—CHILD, MY SPOUSE, MY JOB, LOVE, and SEX—are completely rejected as bad and* passive, *and all of these except CHILD are also* weak *(this may be because CHILD was weak in Eve White and much of the change here is a simple 'flip-flop' of meanings). Note that it is MOTHER in this personality that becomes relatively meaningless; FATHER, on the other hand, stays* good *but shifts completely from* strong *(in Eve White) to* weak— *possible implications of these familial identifications will be considered later. Note also that in this personality LOVE and SEX are closely identified, both as* bad, weak, passive *things,"*

The location of the concepts for Jane on the two occasions are illustrated in Figures 6 and 7.

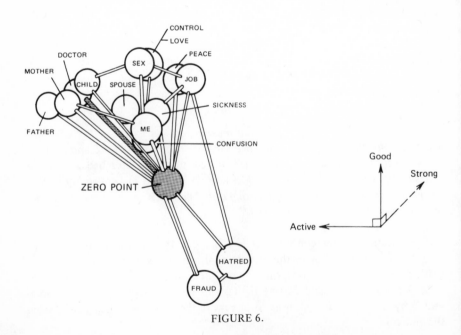

FIGURE 6.

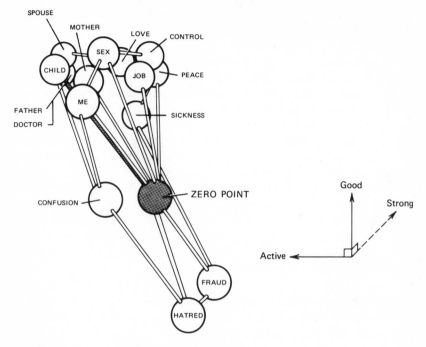

FIGURE 7.

Osgood and Luria describe Jane as follows (1954, pp. 585-586):

"The general characterization is that Jane displays the most 'healthy' meaning pattern, in which she accepts the usual evaluation of concepts by her society yet still maintains a satisfactory evaluation of herself. *MY FATHER, MY MOTHER, MY CHILD, and MY DOCTOR—most of the significant persons in her life—are seen as* good, strong, and active. *The major modes of behavior, PEACE OF MIND, LOVE, SELF-CONTROL, and MY JOB, are seen as equally* good *and* strong, *but* somewhat passive—*as if these ways of behaving and thinking were simply accepted without stress. The two socially agreed-upon evils, HATRED and FRAUD, are put in their proper places. The most significant characteristics of Jane's meaning system, however, are these: The self concept, ME, while still* not strong *(but not* weak, *either) is nearer the* good *and* active *directions of the semantic space; note also the close identification of ME and MENTAL SICK-NESS, which here is* not *an unfavorable concept to her. Her attitude toward her husband, MY SPOUSE, is for the first time meaningful (unlike Eve White) and tending toward the* good, strong, active *directions, like the other significant persons (unlike Eve Black). And LOVE and SEX (quite unlike Eve White) are both favorable and quite closely identified. The changes from testings 1 to 2 are simply such as to strengthen the 'healthy' pattern evident in the first view. ME becomes considerably more* good *and* active; *MY SPOUSE for the first time becomes completely identified connotatively with MY DOCTOR and MY FATHER (and loses its tie with CONFUSION); and LOVE and SEX become*

intimately identified with each other and close in meaning to SELF-CONTROL and PEACE OF MIND."

The reader who has seen the movie or read the book will find these descriptions quite accurate. The attitudes of the three personalities toward these important concepts seem to have been accurately assessed by the semantic differential. Perhaps too accurately. There is some evidence (Norman, 1959) that the responses to the semantic differential are not stable enough for us to expect such accuracy in describing personality; perhaps Osgood and Luria were a little lucky.[2] Nevertheless, their analysis does argue strongly for the utility of the semantic differential. Particularly striking was their speculation (1954, p. 591) that the third personality, Jane—which arose during therapy—was too Pollyanna-like to remain stable. In fact, years later Jane gave way to yet a fourth personality.

8.3 The Own Categories Technique

The semantic differential is typical of categorical rating scale techniques in that the individual devising the technique determines the form of the scale. In contrast, the *own categories technique,* developed by Sherif and his associates, allows the subject to form his own categories; in fact, the number and breadth of these categories are crucial to the assessment of his attitude (Sherif & Hovland, 1953; Reich & Sherif, 1963; Sherif, Sherif, & Nebergall, 1965; Lafave & Sherif, 1968).

The subject is presented with statements concerning a social issue (e.g., desegregation or reapportionment); these statements all express some degree of pro or con attitude. The subject's task is to sort these statements into a number of piles (i.e., categories) in such a way that: (1) the statements in each pile "belong together" and (2) "the piles represent gradations of favorable-unfavorableness toward the" issue (Sherif & Sherif, 1969, p. 351). Furthermore, "great pains are taken *not* to suggest a given number of categories and *not* to suggest that any particular distribution of items into the categories is preferred."

Thus, the task as presented to the subject is one in which the experimenter is interested in finding out something about the attitudes expressed by the statements—not about the attitudes of the subject. (The task is therefore one involving "indirect measurement"; see Chapter IX.) Nevertheless, the subject's response can be used to evaluate an important property of his own attitude. *Subjects who are involved with the issue tend to sort the statements into fewer*

---

[2] Or perhaps the responses of single personalities inhabiting the same body are more stable than are those of normal individuals. Some of this temporal instability in normal individuals' responses may be caused by shifts in mood, whereas such a shift in a person with multiple personalities could result in a change from one personality to another; hence, the responses of a single personality would not vary as much as do those of a single normal individual.

categories than do those who are not involved. This generalization holds, even though subjects who are involved in issues often have much greater factual knowledge about these issues—and hence would be naively expected to make more discriminations among the statements. But they do not. For example, Reich and Sherif (1963) asked two groups of "mature women" (35 to 50 years old) to categorize 60 statements, approximately half of which expressed favorable attitudes toward legislative reapportionment and approximately half of which expressed unfavorable attitudes. One of these groups was composed of active members of the League of Women Voters, which had dedicated its major effort during the year studied to the problem of reapportionment; 74 percent of the women in this group used four or fewer categories in sorting the statements. The other group consisted of a sample of school teachers matched as closely as possible for age and education; only 26 percent of the women in this group used four or fewer categories. Although both groups tended to be favorably disposed toward legislative reapportionment, the League group was much more involved—and much more knowledgeable. Yet, despite this greater knowledgeability, the League women tended to use fewer categories. Similar results have been found using statements about civil rights (Sherif & Hovland, 1953).

After the subject has sorted the statements into categories, it is possible to ask him which categories contain statements that are acceptable to him and which contain statements he finds objectionable. (When this question is asked, the subject is aware that his own attitude is being assessed.) Subjects who are deeply involved in issues tend to find *more* statements objectionable than do subjects who are less involved in the issue. This tendency is part of a "general tendency of highly committed persons to see things in black-and-white terms, and to see more black than white. . . . Politicians sometimes say that people may not be sure what they want, but they are very sure about what they are against" (Sherif & Sherif, 1969, p. 353). Sherif, Sherif, and Nebergall (1965, p. 126) summarize what they found using the own categories technique as follows:

"The behavior measures of attitudes, using these procedures, are the number of categories an individual uses and the distribution of his judgments into them. In general, the more highly involved a respondent is in his stand, the fewer categories he will use, and the mode of his judgments will be at the position most objectionable to him. The less involved the subject, the more categories he will use and the more evenly he will distribute his judgments . . . after all of the material is categorized, the subject may be asked to label his categories as to their acceptability to him."

8.4 The Literal Interpretation Fallacy

Consider a policeman who has taken part in the Sikes and Cleveland (1968) program meant to ease police-community tensions. He is asked to evaluate this program by choosing one of four categories on an evaluative rating scale— "poor," "good," "very good," "excellent." He chooses "good"; does this choice really mean that he regards the program as, literally, "good"?

Suppose he thought the program could best be described as "fair." Faced with the rating scale that Sikes and Cleveland used, he is unable to express this attitude. He may, then, choose "good" in preference to "poor."

Suppose he has a tendency to avoid saying pejorative things about other people or their efforts. No matter how bad he thinks the program is, he must now at least say that it is "good"—if he is to avoid the pejorative label "poor."

Suppose he does not have any very strong opinion about the program; it would then be natural for him to try to avoid using an extreme category to characterize it. Such avoidance leaves him with a choice between saying the program is "good" or "very good."

In short, an individual's response on a rating scale MAY be determined by many factors other than his attitude. His response cannot be interpreted literally. Sikes and Cleveland themselves were aware of this ambiguity and therefore worked out other, more sophisticated, techniques for evaluating police and community attitude (personal communication).

To interpret the response literally is a fallacy. The Sikes and Cleveland scale has been used to illustrate this fallacy because the problems with literal interpretation of responses to this scale are obvious. But all scales are subject to the same problems. For example, a respondent may tell a pollster that he "approves" of his President's policy in a certain country not because he likes the policy at all, but because he feels that it is somehow unpatriotic to "disapprove" of his President—or because he feels that "the President deserves our support" no matter what idiotic course of action he has taken—or because he does not like to say unpleasant things about people and he regards "disapproval" as unpleasant— or even because he suspects that the pollster is compiling information about dissident citizens.

In the above examples, the factors other than the subject's attitude that may influence his response are quite straightforward. Sometimes, however, these factors can be quite subtle. For example, Johnson and Foley (1969) have shown that subjects' rated satisfaction with a teaching device may be manipulated by simply telling them that what they did was a "time-filling" task instead of an educational one.

The principle that rating scale responses cannot be interpreted literally should not be surprising. Since rating scales are usually used as index measures, they must be evaluated in terms of their utility (although it is possible to use rating scales to obtain fundamental measures or functional measures; see Section 7.5 and 7.6). Simply presenting someone with a scale and noting his response to it does not demonstrate the scale's utility. The literal interpretation fallacy lies precisely in believing the individual's response to this scale *in and of itself* provides a certain sort of information. If it does provide information, this fact must be demonstrated—not assumed on the basis of the structure of the scale. Interpreting the response literally involves such an assumption.

8.5 Empirical Justification for Rating Scales

Sometimes rating scales work. They may work in that subjects' responses to rating scales are predictive of future behavior. For example, pollsters use rating scales almost exclusively; their predictions are usually correct, and even when they are wrong, they are wrong only by slight margins, as in the Truman-Dewey election of 1948. (See Abelson, 1968, for a discussion of the remarkable prediction validity of voting surveys; as he argues, even though the voting booth may be "private," people are usually quite frank with their friends and acquaintances about how they plan to vote and how they have voted in the past; they also tend to be quite frank with pollsters.)

Sometimes rating scales may work in that they yield scale values highly similar to those obtained by representational techniques. For example, Thurstone and Chave (1929) proposed that an 11-category rating scale could be used to obtain approximately the same stimulus scale values that are obtained from the comparative judgment technique described in Chapter II. Subjects are asked to place each stimulus to be rated in one of the 11 categories; they are told that these categories should be equally spaced subjectively. The hope of Thurstone and Chave was that the scale values obtained by a rather complex averaging procedure of the categories in which the stimuli are placed would correspond to the scale values obtained by the comparative judgment technique.[3]

Was this hope realized? Unfortunately, the major stimulus domain Thurstone and Chave studied consisted of statements expressing attitudes toward "the church," and these statements were never—to this author's knowledge—scaled by the comparative judgment technique. Instead, Thurstone and Chave were willing to assume rather than prove that the scale values obtained by the two methods would be highly correlated. There is, however, some negative evidence; subjects' own attitudes toward an issue tend to affect their categorical ratings of statements about the issue more than their comparative ratings. There is a slight effect on comparative ratings (Ager & Dawes, 1965; Koslin & Pargament, 1969) in that judges comparing statements with which they disagree tend to make more judgments opposed to consensus ordering than they do when comparing statements with which they agree, but this tendency is not strong enough to have much of an effect on the scale values when the comparative judgment technique is applied. On the other hand, subjects have a tendency to place statements with which they disagree in more extreme categories than they do statements with which they agree (Hovland & Sherif, 1952; Kelley, Hovland,

[3] One reason for using this technique in place of the comparative judgment technique is that fewer judgments must be made. For example, if there are 40 stimuli to be scaled, there are 780 pairs about which subjects could be asked to make comparative judgments, but they need only make 40 judgments in order to place the statements on the 11-category rating scale; Thurstone and Chave argued that many subjects who could be expected to make 40 judgments without an unreasonable amount of fatigue or irritation could not be expected to make 780 judgments without these factors interfering.

Schwartz, & Abelson, 1955), and this *contrast effect* (see Chapter IX, Section 9.3) is strong enough to affect scale values. The *rank order* of the stimuli is generally not affected by the attitude of the raters, but the spacing is.

For the purpose of this book, a study was undertaken to see whether scale values obtained by standard rating scale techniques *can* be highly similar to values obtained by a standard representational technique. The judgment chosen was that of a physical attribute, one which past psychophysical research has indicated may be equivalent psychologically and physically. The attribute chosen was height; Comrey (1950) has shown that ratio judgments of length tend to correspond perfectly to physical ratios, and height is merely vertical length. Hence, psychological height and physical height should be indistinguishable, and we can ask whether the sorts of rating scales used in social psychology can be used to obtain scale values predictive of true height—whether considered physically or psychologically. (A discussion of Comrey's finding and additional analysis of his data may be found in Torgerson, 1958, p.111.)

The five rating scales investigated were those presented in Figure 1. Each of the scales was modified so that it referred to height. For example, scale *a* was changed to read: +3: very tall, +2: moderately tall, +1: tall, −1: short, −2: moderately short, −3: very short. The bipolar adjective pair on scale *b* was "short-tall." Scale *c* was changed to read "extremely tall," "very tall," "tall," and "very short." Scale *d* was unmodified, except that the question read "How tall is this person?" Finally, the verbal labels on scale *e* were changed to "extremely tall," "very tall," "fairly tall," "neither tall nor short," "fairly short," "very short," and "extremely short."

Each of 25 male staff members of the Psychology Department at the University of Oregon was asked to rate the height of all 25, including himself, on the modified scales. These 25 staff members had all known each other for at least two years and were at the University at the time they made the ratings (Spring 1970). Each staff member rated five members on each of the scales. Each rating was made individually on a separate page. The choice of which members were rated by which on which scale was made in such a way that no pair of subjects was rated on a given scale by more than two raters. The order in which the 25 staff members appeared on each rater's form was entirely random.[4]

The design produced five ratings of each staff member on each scale. These ratings were averaged. (Averages on scales *a* and *d* were obtained by averaging the numbers; the averages on scales *b* and *e* were obtained by assigning integer values to the intervals; averages on scale *c* were obtained by assigning the number −2 to the category "very short," the number +1 to the category "tall," the number +2 to the category "very tall," and the number +3 to the category

---

[4] The author is very grateful to his colleagues for their patience and willingness to serve as subjects for this study—and for other equally unorthodox studies as well.

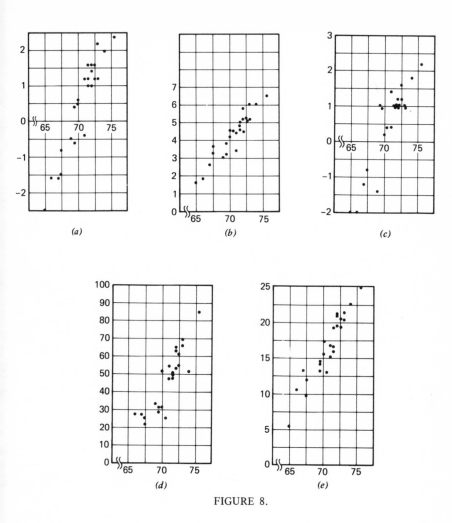

FIGURE 8.

"extremely tall.") These average ratings are plotted against physical height in Figure 8a through 8e. The correlations between the average ratings and physical height range from .88 (for scale d) to .94 (for scales a, b, and e). Scale c, despite its peculiar characteristics, has a correlation of .90.

The intercorrelations between the rating scales are presented in Table 2.

These intercorrelations were factor analyzed (see Chapter IV, Section 4.4). Not surprisingly, the analysis indicated a single factor, one that accounted for 89 percent of the variance (details of the analysis are ommitted). Scores on this factor were estimated for the 25 staff members. These scores are plotted in

Table 2

	Scale *a*	Scale *b*	Scale *c*	Scale *d*	Scale *e*
Scale *a*					
Scale *b*	.90				
Scale *c*	.88	.87			
Scale *d*	.85	.83	.72		
Scale *e*	.92	.91	.84	.91	

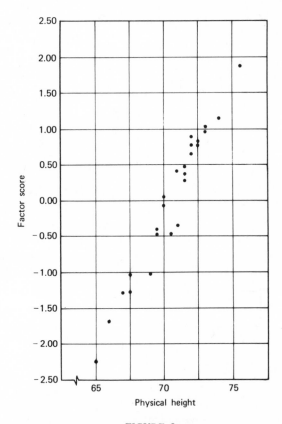

FIGURE 9.

Figure 9 as a function of physical height. The correlation between the factor scores and physical height is .98.[5]

Thus, the rating scale assessment of height produced scale values very highly correlated with the assessment of height by representational techniques (by

[5] It should be noted that this high correlation was obtained after two averaging procedures: the first was the straightforward averaging of five ratings, while the second—obtaining factor scores—involves a weighted average of the five scales. Correlations with individual ratings are much lower.

ruler, or perhaps by ratio estimation). It follows that there is nothing intrinsic about rating scales per se that precludes their use in estimating scale values that will be obtained by representational techniques. It does not, of course, follow that these scales would do as good a job at estimating some representational measure of the attitudes they purport to evaluate.

Sometimes rating scales may work in that they are consistent with one another. That is, results obtained from one type of scale may be highly similar to those obtained from another type of scale. When such similarity is presented as a justification for scale validity, the rationale is basically the same as that used when similarity between rating scale results and representational measurement is presented as a justification, except that the similarity is between two scales considered symmetrically—instead of between one scale (the rating scale) considered as the thing to be evaluated and the other scale (the representational one) considered as the criterion.

Of course, similarity of results is of interest only when the rating scales themselves are intrinsically dissimilar; otherwise, consistency between scales would merely indicate that people respond in similar ways when presented with similar stimuli. The point is that the assessment of the *same* attitudes using *dissimilar* scales should yield similar results, whereas the assessment of different attitudes using similar scales should yield dissimilar results—if similarity of results is to be used as a justification for rating scale use. This rationale for the "convergent validity" of results based on different methods is discussed by Campbell and Fiske (1959) although in the context of personality trait assessment rather than attitude assessment. Such convergent validity is not always found in the field of personality trait assessment (for an amusing study showing lack of convergence, see Goldberg and Werts, 1966). And although theoretically desirable, it is rarely found in the field of attitude assessment. To quote Robinson, Rusk, and Head (1969, p. 19):

". . . the authors find only a couple of personality scales which meet their [Campbell and Fiske's] conditions. To our knowledge, no attitude scales have yet advanced this claim."

8.6 Rating Responses as Constrained Verbalizations

Scott (1968) has proposed that rating scales may also be used as convenient substitutes for *open questions,* such as "what do you think of our President?" Open questions have a number of drawbacks: (1) the answers can be time-consuming for both the respondent and interviewer, (2) the answers may be difficult to interpret, (3) the answers may not be relevant to the concerns of the interviewer (e.g., "I think that he should shave more often"), and (4) because of time limitations, only a limited number may be asked. In contrast, a question demanding a response on a rating scale may be viewed as a *closed question,* that is (Scott, p. 211), "one in which the subject is confronted, not only with a focal object and a dimension of appraisal, but also with a set of categories from which to choose to reply." Thus, the rating scale response itself is a constrained verbalization—one which is less time-consuming, less ambiguous (but see Section 8.4), and guaranteed to be more relevant than a response to an open question. In addition, since rating scale responses are shorter than unconstrained reponses, it is possible to obtain more of them in a given period of time.

8.7 Psychological Justification for Rating Scales

A justification not previously considered is that *certain* rating scales may be compatible with the ways in which the people using them think. For example, people often spontaneously characterize political attitudes in terms of a right-left continuum, and speak of some attitudes as being more extreme or more moderate than others. A rating scale consisting of a line with the labels "left-wing" and "right-wing" at the extreme left and right might be compatible with such people's thinking; they can place attitudes on such a line because they think of such people's attitudes as falling on such a continuum. It is possible that other—more sophisticated—people might think of political beliefs as lying on a circle in which the extreme right and the extreme left converge to a single point of totalitarianism. (Such people may remember that the official policy of the Nazi Party was one of national *socialism.*) These people may then give meaningful responses when asked to locate political attitudes on a circle—again because they think of such attitudes as lying on such a circle.

In fact, there is compelling evidence that some people sometimes think about social phenomena in spatial terms (De Soto, London, & Handel, 1965); such thinking has been termed *spatial paralogic.* For example, the notion that person A is "better than" (or smarter than, healthier than, etc.) person B may be represented spatially by imagining A to be placed above B on a vertical axis; consequently, certain implications among such social relationships are easier to understand than others; the syllogism with premises "A is better than B and B is better than C" is solved with much greater accuracy than is the one with premises "B is worse than A and B is better than C"; this greater accuracy may be predicted from the greater ease of spatial movement in the representation of the first syllogism than in that of the second.

But any good psychological justification for a rating scale technique must avoid the literal interpretation fallacy. That is, it cannot be assumed simply on the basis of the appearance of the scale that it is compatible with the way in which the respondent thinks; there must be some evidence for such compatibility. This evidence may vary anywhere from introspective reports to experimental studies; for example, De Soto, London, and Handel (1965) predicted which syllogisms involving terms like "better than" are difficult and which are easy on the basis of which spatial movements are difficult and which are easy—and their predictions were confirmed. It should be noted that evidence for compatibility does not prove compatibility. Introspective reports may be distorted; the syllogisms that De Soto, London, and Handel thought to be difficult may be difficult for reasons other than those involved with their possible spatial representation. Nevertheless, the point is that someone who argues that a particular rating scale is valid because it is psychologically compatible must have some reasonable answer when confronted with the question "why?".

Psychological compatibility—even if it appears to be established by overwhelming evidence—may be true only for the people on whom the evidence was collected. For example, De Soto, London, and Handel used college students in their studies. College students may not be representative of "people in general," and it is entirely possible that although such students think in terms of spatial paralogic, many people in the general population do not. Or it is possible that a rating scale that is psychologically compatible in one culture would not be in another. Or it is even possible that people's ways of viewing attitudes change across generations or within a generation as a function of age.

There is, however, one very common assumption about the psychology of rating scale use—that *within an individual* the *order* in which he places stimuli on such a scale corresponds to the order in which he views them on the dimension the scale is meant to assess; for example, if an individual checks +3 to indicate his agreement with one statement and +2 to indicate his agreement with a second, it is assumed that he agrees *more* with the first than with the second. People making this assumption (see Dawes-Saraga, 1968; Anderson, 1970) often attempt to phrase their hypotheses—and devise their experiments—in such a way that the crucial aspect of their subjects' rating scale responses is the order in which they place checks on the scale, and only the order. For example, Anderson (1965) has compared two models of impression formation; the first model, which is characterized as a "summation" model, predicts that the more positive information received about somebody the more favorable the impression of him; the second model, which can be termed an "averaging" model, predicts that the favorability of impression is determined by the mean desirability of the information. (This work is also discussed in Section 7.8 of Chapter VII.) Anderson juxtaposes these two models when he writes (1965, p. 394):

"Suppose you considered 'painstaking' to be a moderately desirable trait, and 'well-spoken' to be highly desirable. Would you then like a 'painstaking, well-spoken' person more than a 'well-spoken' person?"

To answer this question, Anderson asked subjects to rate people who are well-spoken and painstaking, and people who are just well-spoken. He found that people to whom a single highly desirable (or undesirable) trait is ascribed are rated as more desirable (or undesirable) than are those to whom both a highly polarized and a less polarized trait are ascribed. Thus, he managed to compare the conflicting models of impression formation in such a way that he only had to pay attention to the order in which people are rated on a rating scale. Dawes (Dawes-Saraga, 1968) has shown that many additional models of impression formation can be tested and compared solely on the basis of the order of rating scale responses. (It should be noted that Fishbein and Hunter, 1964, conducted a study similar to Anderson's and found diametrically opposed results.)

The assumption concerns only *intraindividual* comparisons; that is, there is no assumption that if individual 1 assigns the number +3 to indicate his agreement with statement *a* and then individual 2 assigns the number +2 then individual 1 agrees more than does individual 2. Furthermore, the intraindividual assumption is made in the absence of any formal evidence. It seems very compelling, however, that individuals who are familiar with number and position through years of schooling should use at least the ordinal properties of rating scales to reflect their feelings about the way things are ordered.

8.8 Common Problems in Rating Scale Construction

Consider the subject who is asked to indicate his agreement or disagreement with the first statement presented in Figure 1*a:* "Sciences like chemistry, physics, and medicine have carried men very far, but there are many important things that can never possibly be understood by the human mind." Suppose the subject believes that there *are* "many important things that can never possibly be understood by the human mind," and in addition he believes that sciences like physics and chemistry have *not* "carried men very far"—but in fact have led to nuclear weaponry, overpopulation, pollution, and general lousiness in the quality of life. How is he to respond? If he agrees, he is agreeing to the proposition that sciences like physics and chemistry have been beneficial; if he disagrees, he is disagreeing with the proposition that many important things cannot be understood by the human mind. No matter what category of agreement or disagreement he chooses, he is committing himself to a proposition in which he does not believe. Or consider the same subject faced with the second statement in Figure 1*a:* "Most people don't realize the extent to which their lives are governed by secret plots hatched in hidden places." If the subject indicates strong disagreement with this statement, does he mean that most people really *do* realize that their lives are controlled by secret plots hatched in hidden places? If he believes that people's lives are not so governed, he might find himself forced to agree strongly with the statement; people do not realize this, because it is not true. But he may well have serious qualms about endorsing the statement in order to indicate his disagreement with the dependent clause about secret plots, and his qualms will be well taken because the psychologist will interpret agreement to be indicative of a paranoid attitude.

"Double-barreled" statements such as the first and statements involving dependent clauses such as the second can often create serious problems—both for the subject responding to them on a rating scale and for the psychologist attempting to interpret his response. For many years (Wang, 1932) psychologists have been urged to write items that are simple and short when they construct rating scales. The problems with such statements (e.g., "the radicals should be shot") is that the implications of agreeing or disagreeing with them are often quite transparent to the subject, and he may then choose to agree or disagree for reasons other than that of expressing what he believes to be his attitude. (And again, literal interpretation would be a fallacy.) Furthermore, some important attitudes are intrinsically complex and cannot be expressed by a short, simple statement. (See Rorer, 1965, for a discussion of problems in writing attitude items.)

In addition to the problem of ambiguities in statement construction, there is that of ambiguity in the rating scale itself. Consider, for example, the rating scale used by Sikes and Cleveland (Figure 1c). As was pointed out in Section 8.4, the asymmetrical nature of this scale makes it very difficult to interpret subjects' responses. But should scales always be symmetrical? If so, symmetrical about what? And how is distance from this point of symmetry determined? In fact, there are situations where symmetrical rating scales might not even be desirable; for example, extensive experience in evaluating teaching at the University of Michigan[6] has indicated that students are loathe to say that a teacher is anything less than "good"—at least they were prior to the protest movements that started in the late 1960s. Hence, course evaluation scales were constructed that centered around the category "good," with the other categories being "superior," "very good," "average," and "poor." This asymmetrical category scheme led to a somewhat symmetrical distribution of responses, which was thought desirable in order to differentiate among teachers. Had the scale been centered around "average," almost all the ratings may have fallen in the upper two categories.[7]

Another common problem in rating scale construction is that of *confounding* two or more dimensions in a single scale; these dimensions may be either explicit or implicit. For example, suppose a subject is asked to rate a person or a group of people on a bipolar scale defined by the adjectives *generous-stingy* or by the adjectives *extravagant-thrifty*. Both adjective pairs refer to a dimension of "looseness" versus "tightness" with regard to spending money. Both also, however, have evaluative connotations; thrift and generosity are good, whereas stinginess and extravagance are bad; thus, the first pair confounds the loose versus tight dimension with the evaluative dimension in such a way that the loose end of the loose-tight dimension is identified with the good end of the good-bad dimension, whereas the second adjective pair confounds the two

---

[6] Personal experience.

[7] I state "may" because I do not know of any good evidence one way or the other. It is possible that if these labels had been arranged differently on the rating scale, then the students would check the same labels even though such checking meant checking at different locations on the scale; it is also possible that the students would check at the same points on the scale, even though such behavior meant checking different labels; most likely, some combination of these two changes would occur.

dimensions in the other direction. For a full discussion of such confounding, see Peabody (1968). Again, however, a blanket prohibition against such confounding may be ill advised; there may be domains in which confounding is "natural," or even necessary; for example, a dimension running from "hippy" to "straight" may confound a number of dimensions ranging from appearance to political philosophy (and may be confounded with evaluation—in a different direction for different raters); yet it may be an extremely valuable dimension for rating impressions of young people.

A final common problem is that of *response bias*. Consider, for example, the rating scale meant to assess "authoritarianism"; statements expressing authoritarian attitudes are rated from −3 to +3 to indicate the rater's disagreement or agreement with them. Because all the statements express authoritarian attitudes, responding in an authoritarian manner is confounded with responding in an agreeing manner. And psychologists have discovered that many people tend to agree with statements. (It has been found, for example, that many people will agree with both a statement and its "opposite"—although the definition of "opposite" is not always clear.) Thus, the individual who is rated high on authoritariansim because of his response to these items may just be someone who tends to agree a lot—either because he is wishy-washy, or because he adopts a strategy of saying "yes" whenever he is unsure, or even because he tends to misread statements in such a way that they conform to his own attitudes. As Rorer (1965) and Rorer and Goldberg (1965) note, however, there is little evidence that people differ reliably in their tendency to agree—that is, there is little evidence that this tendency constitutes an important *interindividual* difference between people.

Faced with this bias toward agreement, many psychologists have attempted to construct scales in such a way that the attitude being assessed is expressed by agreement half the time and by disagreement half the time. Again, however, there is the problem that in some situations the confounding of attitude with response bias is reasonable; for example, "authoritarianism" refers in part to an attitude of agreement with what those in authority assert. How can authoritarianism then be assessed by constructing statements with which the authoritarian disagrees? This problem is particularly tricky, because it is possible for an individual with authoritarian attitudes to hold contradictory beliefs (e.g., that Jews are too clannish and that they should stay among their own people). For a fuller discussion of the problems of response bias, see Rorer (1965), Peabody (1966), and Webb et al. (1966, pp. 19-20).

In this section, four common problems of rating scale construction have been briefly outlined: ambiguity of statements, ambiguity of scales, confounding, and response bias. There are many other problems as well, all which stem from the fact that the response of a subject to a rating scale is basically ambiguous. As was emphasized in Section 8.4, the literal interpretation of such responses is a fallacy. This section has presented four problems that may contribute to difficulty in interpreting rating scale responses, even when it is kept in mind that these responses should not be interpreted literally. Insofar as these problems can be surmounted, interpretation of the responses becomes somewhat less ambiguous; it can, however, never be completely unambiguous.

QUESTIONS

1. Suppose that a group of patients rate the concepts used by Osgood and Luria on the semantic differential. Consider the distance between any two such concepts. Suppose the concepts are located in the semantic space separately for each individual and then the average distance between these two concepts is computed. Demonstrate by example that this average may be different from the distance that would be obtained if the patients' responses on each dimension were first averaged and a single semantic space was constructed.

2. Conduct an experiment in which your subjects are asked to rate concepts on the semantic differential and then asked to make proximity judgments concerning the concepts—for example, they might be presented with triples of concepts located in a triangle and asked to indicate which two concepts are the most alike to them and which two are the least alike. Are the distances in the semantic space compatible with proximity judgements? If so, how compatible are they? Should they be? If no relationship were found, would doubt be cast on Osgood and Luria's suggestion that these distances correspond to "difference in meaning"?

3. The subject's task in the own categories technique is to sort statements into a number of piles in such a way that: (a) the statements in each pile "belong together" and (b) the piles represent gradations of favorableness-unfavorableness toward the issue to which the statements refer. Suppose subjects were given only the fist instruction—that is, to sort the statements into piles that "belong together." In what ways would the piles obtained from this single instruction differ from those obtained under the ordinary instructions? Or would they? What sort of information could be obtained by using only the first instruction that could not be obtained by using the standard instructions?

4. The standard procedure used by Sherif and his associates for finding which statements their subjects reject is to ask them to state which piles (categories) they find objectionable. Suppose subjects were asked simply to state which statements they find objectionable without first sorting them into piles. Would the same statements be rejected?

5. The Johnson and Foley study demonstrated that telling someone that a given procedure was "educational" or "a time filler" can influence his rating of that procedure. Can it not be argued that actually his attitude has been influenced? And therefore the rating he gives may be quite valid?

6. Repeat the height study using two other physical variables. Construct a rating scale that you think would do a good job of assessing the first but not

the second, and one you think would do a good job of assessing the second but not the first.

7. Construct two rating scales for assessing political attitude, one consisting of a line running from "left-wing" to "right-wing" and one consisting of a circle in which "left-wing" and "right-wing" meet at a point labeled "totalitarianism." Ask subjects to rate statements on these scales at two different times. On which scale are subjects more consistent? On which do they agree more with each other?

8. Anderson, Dawes, and others are willing to make the *intraindividual* assumption that the order in which people place objects or statements on rating scales represents the order in which they perceive them—for example, a person who rates agreement with statement *a* as +3 and with statement *b* as +2 agrees more with statement *a* than with statement *b*. It is possible to make the dual assumption, which is the *interindividual* assumption, that the individual who rates the object or statement as more extreme perceives it as more extreme—for example, if individual *a* gives a +3 rating to indicate his agreement with a statement and individual *b* gives a +2 rating, then individual *a* agrees more with the statement than does individual *b*. Compare the two assumptions. Which is more compelling?

9. Devise a study to evaluate the intraindividual assumption.

10. Why should we have fewer concerns about statement and response mode ambiguities when dealing with representational measurement techniques than when dealing with an index measurement technique such as the common rating scale?

11. Construct two scales to evaluate teaching effectiveness (or a similar variable) in such a way that the scales are physically identical and have the same verbal labels but the labels are located at different points on the scales. Do subjects tend to agree on the physical placement of their ratings, or on the verbal labels associated with the ratings?

12. In a famous study discussed in Chapter V, Section 5.2, LaPiere (1934) obtained verbal replies of hotel, motel, and restaurant owners to the question: "Will you accept members of the Chinese race as guests in your establishment?" The overwhelming response was "no." Yet in traveling around the country with a Chinese couple, he and the couple were refused service at such establishments only once and given service on 251 occasions. LaPiere concludes that verbal responses to such questions are of dubious value. He writes (p. 237):

"The questionnaire is cheap, easy, and mechanical. The study of human behavior is time consuming, intellectually fatiguing, and depends for its success upon the ability of the investigator. The former method gives quantitative results, the latter mainly qualitative. Quantitive measurements are quantitatively

accurate; qualitative evaluations are always subject to the errors of human judgment. Yet it would seem far more worthwhile to make a shrewd guess regarding that which is essential than to accurately measure that which is likely to prove quite irrelevant."

Discuss this quote.

IX

Indirect Evaluation
of Attitude

9.1 Introduction

When most of the techniques presented thus far in this book are applied, the subject is aware that his attitude is being assessed. This awareness may affect his behavior. For example, he may wish to appear unprejudiced when responding to a social distance scale concerning blacks (but, nevertheless, avoid associating with blacks). Or he may wish to appear reasonably healthy psychologically when rating the concept "me" on the semantic differential. Or he may state that he prefers to have two children when he is being interviewed by a college student, because he believes college students are opposed to larger families, and he wishes to avoid displeasing the interviewer.

Responses that are determined partially or wholly by knowledge of being an object of study have been termed *reactive* by Campbell and Stanley (1963). The subject is reacting to the fact of being observed. His responses may then be different from those that would occur if he were placed in the same situation without the knowledge that his behavior is being studied by somone else. Clearly, such reactive responses pose a problem for the psychologist or other social scientist interested in the subject's reaction to the situation per se. [But there are some psychologists (e.g., Orne, 1962) who are interested in studying reactivity per se—i.e., in studying how it is that people react to the fact of being an object of psychological investigation.]

Campbell (1950) has urged the development of attitude assessment techniques that will not elicit reactive responses. He writes (p. 15):

"In the problem of assessing social attitudes, there is a very real need for instruments which do not destroy the natural form of the attitude in the process of describing it. There are also situations in which one would like to assess 'prejudice' without making respondents self-conscious or aware of the intent of the study."

120

Thus, Campbell is expressing the need for techniques that do not involve the subject's knowledge that his attitude is being evaluated; such techniques have come to be termed *indirect*. A variety of these techniques will be presented in this chapter. (A much more extensive presentation may be found in Webb, Campbell, Schwartz and Sechrest, 1966). The techniques will be categorized in terms of whether the subject is entirely unaware that he is even being observed, or whether he is aware that he is being observed but not aware that his attitudes are being assessed. At the end of the chapter, there will be a discussion of the ethical problems raised by such indirect techniques. Do psychologists really have the right to evaluate people's attitudes without letting the people know that they are being evaluated?

9.2 Techniques in Which the Subject Is Unaware that He Is Being Observed

A classic technique in which the subject is unaware that his attitude is being evaluated is the one devised by Melton (1933, 1936) to assess museum visitors' attitudes toward various displays. He observed the number of times the tiles in front of each exhibit had to be replaced. His basic idea was that the greater the replacement frequency, the more popular the exhibit. In addition, however, he controlled for the biases of museum visitors that might tend to cause certain tiles to be replaced irrespective of the attraction of the exhibit in front of the tiles; for example, visitors have a "right-turning bias" in that they tend to turn toward the right after entering through the door of a museum room; visitors tend to drag their feet more toward the end of their museum visit, and so on. Once corrections are made for these extraneous factors that wear down tiles, the replacement rate can be used as an indirect measure of interest.

A more recent indirect technique is Milgram's *letter drop* procedure (Milgram, Mann, & Harter, 1965) for assessing the political attitude of people in a given location. A post office box is hired to receive mail for various bogus political organizations. Each of these organizations has a title that clearly implies a certain political philosophy (e.g., "Young Communist League," "Citizens Against Gun Control"). Stamped letters addressed to these organizations are then "dropped" in various places within the community—such as telephone booths, on the street, in department stores. The relative frequency with which the letters are picked up and mailed is used as an indicator of the positive feeling in the location toward the philosophy expressed in the title of the organization.

A final technique discussed in this section is that of *automobile observation*. The characteristics of people's automobiles often indicate something about their attitude; for example, people do or do not display bumper stickers that express certain political or philosophical positions; they do or do not comply with certain state or local laws concerning inspection and registration; the tires are generally good or smooth, and so on. Wrightsman (1969) used automobile observation as a way of assessing the attitudes toward "law and order" of the supporters of George Wallace's 1968 Presidential candidacy. He was teaching in Nashville, Tennessee on election day in 1968; on that day, he had his students observe the frequency with which automobiles bearing Wallace stickers, Nixon stickers, and Humphrey stickers also displayed an automobile tax sticker that each automobile owner was supposed to have bought and put on his automobile by November 2. Failure to buy the sticker was a violation of the law. Thus, Wrightsman's study was generated by "a curiosity as to whether supporters of Wallace were, in fact, more law abiding than were supporters of the other candidates" (p. 17). This curiosity was aroused because Wallace had made the need for "law and order" one of his campaign issues. In actuality, the proportion of automobiles with Wallace stickers that failed to display the required tax stickers was larger that either the proportion of automobiles with Nixon stickers that failed or the proportion of automobiles with Humphrey stickers that failed (and also larger than a control group of automobiles that displayed either no campaign sticker at all or a sticker for someone not running–e.g., McCarthy or Snoopy). Of the Wallace automobiles, 25 percent failed to display the tax sticker, whereas only 14 percent of the Nixon automobiles and 14 percent of the Humphrey automobiles failed to do so.

Of course, there may be a number of extraneous reasons why the Wallace automobiles failed to display the sticker–reasons that have nothing to do with the attitude of Wallace supporters toward obeying the law. For example, the Wallace supporters may have been less wealthy and therefore less able to buy the stickers. It turned out, however, that even when cars were divided into those that were "new" (1964 models on) and those that were "old," the same difference among supporters of the three candidates was found. Wrightsman presents further evidence that the difference he found is due to attitude toward law and order when he cites a personal communication from John McCarthy that (p. 22) "observers at a Nashville intersection with a stop sign . . . recorded the percentage and types of cars failing to stop. A significantly higher percentage of cars with Wallace bumper stickers failed to stop."

9.3 Techniques in Which the Subject Is Aware That He Is Being Observed, but not That His Attitude Is Being Assessed

The subject knows he is an object of study, but he does not know that his attitude is being assessed–or, alternatively, he has no control over his responses on which this assessment is based. For example, the subject whose attitude is being assessed by the own categories technique (Section 8.3 of Chapter VIII) believes he is presenting the experimenter with judgments about the attitude statements he is sorting instead of with information about himself. Or certain responses over which the subject has no control, such as physiological reactions, may be observed. For example, people's pupils tend to dilate when they observe a stimulus in which they are particularly interested (Hess, 1965).

The most dramatic investigations of pupil dilation as an indicator of interest have dealt with sexual interest. Hess, Seltzer, and Shlien (1965) investigated the pupil dilation of five heterosexual and five overtly homosexual males when viewing pictures of nude or partially nude males and females; the average pupil dilation (as opposed to "control" pictures) when viewing the female pictures minus the average dilation when viewing the male pictures was computed separately for each subject; all five heterosexual males showed a greater difference in average dilation than did any of the homosexual males (although one of the homosexuals did show a positive difference—i.e., a greater average dilation when viewing females than when viewing males). In a similar but larger study, Atwood and Howell (1971) investigated the pupil dilations of 10 normals and 10 pedophiliacs (child molesters) when viewing nude or partially nude pictures of adult females and young girls. (All the subjects were prisoners; the pedophiliacs had all molested young girls, but none had been guilty of physical abuse.) The average change in pupil dilation when looking at the pictures as opposed to blurred slides is presented in Table 1 for each of the 20 subjects separately. All but one (S7) of the pedophiliacs dilated more to pictures of young girls, and all but one (S19) of the normals dilated more to pictures of adult females. Concerning the single deviant pedophiliac, the authors write (1971, p. 116):

"This S reported that he molested girls only after drinking large amounts of alcohol. Possibly his choice of young girls as a sexual target was due to lack of discrimination rather than a preference. . . . He was the only S who blamed alcohol for his deviant act."

Although there is support for the contention that peoples' pupils tend to dilate when they are looking at an object of interest, it should be emphasized that there are many other factors which tend to cause pupil dilation or constriction; the most obvious is light intensity, but there are also many subtle ones—for example, a subject looking at a boring stimulus may actually be thinking about a previous one that he found exciting, thereby causing his pupils to dilate. Also, it is not clear whether stimuli that are distasteful or repulsive cause pupil constriction, or dilation. For a review of the complex methodological issues involved in using pupil dilation as an indirect indicator of attitude, see Woodmansee (1970).

Another classic technique in which the subject's attitude is evaluated without his knowledge is the *error-choice* method devised by Hammond (1948). The subject is presented with a series of multiple-choice items purporting to assess his factual knowledge about various domains. Many of these items do concern facts and do have correct answers among the response alternatives. Several of the items, however, have only incorrect or ambiguous response alternatives, and they are devised so that the subject's choice among these is indicative of his attitude. For example, an item might read: "On the average, nonsmokers live (*a.* 5, *b.* 15)

Table 1   Mean Pupil Changes (mm) When Data Are Grouped According to
           Slide Content[a]

Content	Adult Females	Young Females
Pedophiliacs		
1	+15	+38
2	− 2	+22
3	− 7	+17
4	− 6	+ 6
5	− 5	+31
6	−11	+24
7	− 2	−10
8	−10	+25
9	− 4	+28
10	+ 6	+29
$\overline{X}$	− 2.6	+21.0
Control		
11	+28	+25
12	+18	+ 5
13	+29	− 8
14	+21	+14
15	+25	+ 5
16	+21	− 7
17	+22	− 6
18	+35	+ 3
19	−26	0
20	+16	− 8
$\overline{X}$	+18.9	+ 2.3
	$t = 4.51^{b}$	$t = 3.43^{b}$

[a]The millimeter (mm) changes do *not* refer to actual changes in the pupil but instead to changes on a 24-inch television screen on which the pupil was projected. Since the detailed specifications of the projection apparatus are no longer available (Atwood, personal communication), it is not possible to convert to the number of millimeters in actual pupil dilation.

[b]$p < .01$.

years longer than do heavy smokers." The correct number of years is 10. A choice of 5 would be interpreted as indicating a favorable attitude toward smoking, while a choice of 15 would be interpreted as indicating an unfavorable attitude toward smoking. Or an item might read: "In general, the eastern European Communist countries have been (*a.* better than, *b.* worse than) average in honoring their international commitments." Here, the supposedly factual question calls for a value judgment on the part of the subject—a requirement that may well escape the subject's notice when the item is embedded in a number of purely factual ones.

Notice that certain assumptions are involved in interpreting the subject's "error-choice"; for example, underestimating the adverse effect of cigarette smoking on longevity indicates a favorable attitude toward cigarettes only granting the assumption that the subject making this error has a favorable attitude toward longevity; similarly, the belief that Communist countries generally fulfill their commitments indicates a favorable attitude toward these countries only if the respondent has a favorable attitude toward fulfilling commitments. In his initial paper presenting the method, Hammond (1948) presents data that assumptions like these are quite reasonable—*at least for the items he tested.* The items were meant to indicate attitude toward labor unions and toward Communism; businessmen and union members responded in radically different ways. (The study was completed shortly after World War II, before many laborers had become anti-Communist.)

There are also a number of indirect techniques similar to the own categories technique in that the subject is asked to rate, compare, or generate attitude statements supposedly to convey information about these statements, but with the ulterior purpose of evaluating the subject's own attitude. For example, Selltiz, Edrich, and Cook (1965) proposed that subjects' attitudes can be assessed by the way in which they rate opinion statements on standard rating scales. Their proposal was based on the finding of Hovland and Sherif (1952) that people with a pro or con attitude tend to "contrast" statements expressing an opposing attitude—that is, they tend to give such statements a more extreme rating on a rating scale than do neutralists or people agreeing with the statements. Selltiz, Edrich, and Cook showed that subjects who belong to groups that generally entertain prejudiced or nonprejudiced attitudes toward blacks rated statements about blacks and about civil rights differently; consistent with the earlier findings, the subjects belonging to the prejudiced groups tended to rate statements that were pro black or pro civil rights as more extreme than did the subjects who belonged to the nonprejudiced groups, and vice versa. The authors did not, however, evaluate how well this phenomenon would allow them to predict the group membership of the subject doing the rating.

In a similar vein, Ager and Dawes (1965) have shown that pro and anti subjects tend to differ in their paired comparisons of pro and anti statements; that is, when subjects are asked to state which of two statements is more pro, those who are themselves anti are more likely to make a choice different from the consensus choice than are those who are themselves pro, and vice versa. Again, however, the authors did not evaluate how well this phenomenon would allow them to predict the group membership of the subject making the paired comparison.

Ager and Dawes interpreted their results as meaning that people with a pro or an anti attitude "fail to discriminate" between attitudes with which they disagree more than between attitudes with which they agree. More recently, Koslin and Pargament (1969), replicating the Ager and Dawes finding in a different attitude domain, have challenged this interpretation. These authors argue that if the results were caused by failure to discriminate, then pro's should make more intransitive judgments (statement a ordered above statement b, statement b ordered above statement c, yet statement c ordered above statement *a*) when judging anti statements than do anti's, and—once again—vice versa. Such an effect was not obtained. The conclusion of Koslin and Pargament was that the Ager and Dawes finding referred simply to "disagreement." For the purpose of indirect assessment of attitude, it is irrelevant whether this difference between pro's and anti's is due to a discrimination failure or to simple disagreement; the point is that they make these comparative judgments differently, and hence a judgment that is different from the consensus judgment can be indicative of the individual's attitude.[1]

Another indirect technique involving attitude statements was devised by Dawes, Singer, and Lemons (1971), who found that the contrast effect referred to above occurs not only in rating attitude statements but also in generating them. People who have a position on an issue generate more extreme statements when they are asked to write those that will be endorsed by the typical person with whom they disagree than when they are asked to write those that will be endorsed by the typical person with whom they agree. The effect is quite striking. For example, prior to the 1968 elections both Wallace supporters and supporters of the write-in protest were asked to write statements that would be endorsed by the typical member of each group; the writer of such statements can be classified as a Wallace supporter or protester himself with roughly 80 percent accuracy by a single judge; accuracy based on a number of judges is even higher. The statements written by one Wallace supporter and one supporter of the write-in protest are presented in Table 2. These were two subjects whose own attitudes were readily classified by the judges in the Dawes et al. studies.

Subjects tend to have even less control over their physiological responses than over their verbal ones (although there may be some exceptions). Hence, such physiological responses as pupillary expansion—discussed above—can be used as indirect indicators of attitude. Another rather striking physiological response is the *galvanic skin response* (GSR), which tends to occur when a person is anxious or aroused. This response is a change in the electrical conduction of the skin, which can be brought about by sweating, increased or decreased capillary flow, and so on; generally, the response manifests itself by a drop in skin resistance—as measured by standard electrical techniques. Cooper and Pollock (1959) have discovered that such responses occur in prejudiced individuals when *favorable* remarks are made about the objects of their prejudice.

[1] It should be noted that Koslin and Pargament found that the number of intransitive judgments was related to involvement; uninvolved subjects made more intransitive judgments than did involved subjects; hence intransitivity may be an index of involvement. Braatz (1970) found that schizophrenic hospital patients made more intransitive judgments than did other hospital patients when judging which of two activities was more aversive (e.g., walking a mile when it is 15 degrees below zero, licking stamps for 1,000 letters) or which of two was more pleasurable (e.g., getting an unexpected bonus, having a strong personal attachment for someone). While Braatz interprets his results in terms of the "cognitive slippage" of his schizophrenic subjects, an alternative explanation is that they were simply less involved in such activities than were the other hospital patients; these activities may have a highly hypothetical quality for people unfortunate enough to be hospitalized with a "schizophrenic" label.

Table 2

Statements written by a Wallace supporter

Wallace statements	Write-in protest statements
Executive orders and bureau directives should not be permitted to control areas of operation granted the state by the Constitution of the U.S.	Writing in McCarthy will give public declaration that all other candidates fail to embody American ideals.
Judicial "rewriting" of the U.S. should be curtailed—legislative lawmaking should prevail.	No ideology is worthy of war.
Peaceful resistance and demonstrations should not remove or restrict freedoms of any other persons—including freedom of HEARING at public gatherings.	Gregory is the only candidate who represents the Afro-American interest in the election.
Discrimination should be illegal— integration should occur on a voluntary basis so as to limit hostilities.	McCarthy is a candidate who has not sold himself to the Hawks as have Humphrey, Nixon and Wallace.

Statements written by a write-in protest supporter

Wallace statements	Write-in protest statements
More law and order.	Provide the American public with leaders chosen by the public instead of by political party machinery.
Win militarily in Viet Nam.	Withdraw from Vietnam as quickly as possible.
Prosecute all dissidents and revolutionists.	Defend American freedom to dissent and disagree.
Return power to the states.	Provide for equal opportunity for all Americans regardless of race, creed, color, or economic state.

"Display of excessive affectivity in response to a complementary [sic] description of a national or ethnic group is predictive of an antipathetic prejudicial-attitude toward that group. . . . A relatively great GSR to a complimentary verbal description of a national or ethnic group is predictive of a relatively low attitude scale position for that group" (Cooper & Pollock, 1959, p. 242).

Another indirect technique, *partner preference,* has been devised by Rokeach and Mezei (1966). This technique consists of having confederates (stooges) express certain attitudes and then asking the subject to indicate a social preference for one or more of these confederates. For example, some confederates may express left-wing attitudes and others right-wing attitudes, and then the subject is asked to choose which confederates he wishes to join him for coffee. Of course, since the confederates may differ in their intrinsic attractiveness as social partners, it is necessary that this factor be "controlled" in some manner; the confederates may, for example, be matched on probability of being chosen when neither expresses an attitude; or when the purpose of the technique is to assess the attitude of a group of people instead of a single person, different confederates may adopt different positions with different members of this group.

The best-known study using partner preference as an attitude assessment technique (Rokeach & Mezei, 1966) contrasted shared belief versus skin color as determinants of such preference. Subjects interacted with four confederates, two of whom were black and two of whom were white; the situation was arranged so that a controversial topic was discussed; by a prearranged schedule, one black and one white confederate agreed with whatever views the subject expressed, and one white and one black confederate disagreed. The subject then indicated a partner preference for two of the four confederates.

Three distinct preference situations were studied. The first used Michigan State students in 1961 as subjects, the second used Michigan State students in the school year 1962-1963, and the third used applicants for jobs at the two Michigan mental hospitals (the jobs were those of custodian, laundry worker, attendant, and recreation director). The subjects in the first two situations were all white, whereas half the subjects in the third situation were white and half were black. In the first two situations, the subject was chosen as "chairman" of a discussion group that would discuss a controversial issue—for the purpose of enlightening the experimenter about student views on that issue; the subject and the confederates were then told that the experimenter wished to interview each separately, and the subject—as chairman—was asked to indicate which two confederates he would like to have join him for coffee while the other two were interviewed. In the job applicant situation, the subject was drawn into a conversation with the confederates concerning strict versus lenient policies toward mental patients, and he was later asked during his job interview which two of the four he would prefer to have as co-workers.

The results of the partner preferences are presented in Table 3. The columns of this table indicate the type of pairs chosen—either for coffee or as co-workers; the S's and O's indicate whether the chosen partner was of the "same" or of the "other" race, and the pluses and minuses indicate whether he agreed or disagreed with the subject's stand on the issue discussed; the numbers indicate the frequencies with which each column choice was made.

Table 3

	S+O+	S−O−	S+S−	O+O−	S+O−	S−O+
Situation 1 (Campus 1961)	4	1	2	1	3	9
Situation 2 (Campus 1962-1963)	13	0	3	3	15	14
Situation 3 (Job application)	30	3	2	3	4	8
Total	47	4	7	7	22	31

Of the people chosen, 118 had the same skin color as the subject, while 118 had a different skin color; in contrast, 161 had agreed with the subject and 75 had disagreed. Rokeach and Mezei interpret these results as strong support for the hypothesis that partner preference is based more on shared belief than on shared race. But they did not analyze the choices of the pairs considered as pairs instead of as two separate partners. As has been pointed out elsewhere (Dawes, 1966), such an analysis indicates a strong tendency for the subjects to choose one member of the same race and one member of the other race. Consider, for example, choices where one partner agreed and one partner disagreed; these could be either choices of two people who are the same race (SS or OO) or two people of different races (SO or OS); 53 of the 67 choices were of racially mixed pairs. Consider, also, the choices of the college students among racially mixed pairs; if Rokeach and Mezei are right that shared belief is the main determinant of such choices, it would follow that S+O+ pairs would be chosen with much greater frequency than the other racially mixed pairs (S−O−, S+O−, and S−O+); yet, combining situations 1 and 2, both the S+O− and S−O+ choices outnumber the S+O+ choices. Clearly, the choice of these students involved an avoidance of forming racially homogeneous groups—that is, an avoidance of segregation. The subjects were responsive to skin color.

9.4 The Ethical Problems of Indirect Assessment

If—for whatever reason—an ordinary citizen wishes to keep his political beliefs private, we would be hesitant to tap his telephone, bug his martini olive, or hire a professional detective to discover these beliefs. And if we did any of these things, he would be furious. Yet the techniques presented in this chapter are designed not only to assess political attitudes without the knowledge of the person being assessed (and perhaps against his will), but even racial and sexual attitudes as well. Is such assessment ethical?

The question has no simple answer. There are some situations where such assessment is clearly ethical; if, for example, a man comes to a psychologist for help with personality problems, then it is not only ethical but desirable for the psychologist to assess the man's attitudes by whatever means available. Consider, however, job applicants in the Rokeach and Mezei (1966) study. They were not seeking help concerning their racial attitudes; they were seeking employment. Did Rokeach and Mezei have the right to study their attitudes in such a situation? without even informing them then or later that they were in a psychological experiment? These questions are not purely hypothetical; the Rokeach and Mezei study in fact aroused negative comment (*cf.* Miller, 1966; Maloney, 1966). The study even led one critic (Standen, 1966, p. 1456) to conclude:

"I hope that we will never see government by, or relying too much on the advice of, behavioral scientists. I would not trust my civil liberties to such people."

Or consider subjects whose attitudes are assessed by the error-choice technique. If they believe the deception that all the questions have a correct response alternative, they may come away from the testing situation with a new fund of misinformation; for example, the person with the favorable attitude toward smoking may now believe that it only shortens life 5 years on the average, while the person with an unfavorable attitude may now believe that figure is 15 years. Conceivably, this misinformation could have an adverse effect on these people—for example, in terms of motivating them to smoke or quit. Is it ethical for the psychologist to reinforce misinformed belief?

The error-choice technique points out another problem inherent in some of the indirect assessment methods. Contrary to what the psychologist says, there are no correct answers to some of the questions. The psychologist lies. Should a psychologist—who is often regarded as an authority figure, who is a member of the psychological profession—be permitted to lie? The lie may be a white lie, but it is about psychological matters. Does the public not have a right to think that psychologists speak the truth when they talk about psychology? Pragmatically, will it not hurt other psychologists if it is known that some psychologists lie?[2]

One possible answer to these questions is that people are manipulating other people and lying to them all the time. The only difference between an ordinary interaction in everyday life and an indirect attitude assessment method of the psychologist is that the latter is more systematic. Consider, for example, the use of pupillary expansion as a method of assessing interest. Many shrewd salesmen and able seducers have known for years that pupillary dilation is indicative of interest. Is the psychologist to suppress his knowledge of what such dilation means? We see nothing wrong in observing that certain people are anxious or assured when giving public speeches, or when attending a party, or when engaged in intimate conversation. What is then wrong with observing that a certain man's pupils expand more when he looks at men than when he looks at women?

No answers to these ethical problems are proposed here. The reader should be aware, however, that these problems exist. And as indirect assessment techniques become more sophisticated, the problems may grow increasingly difficult.

---

[2] Ethical objections to the error-choice technique may be ameliorated to a certain extent by "debriefing" the subjects after their attitudes have been assessed—that is, by explaining the technique to them. This debriefing procedure, however, raises new problems of its own; to quote Robinson, Rusk, and Head (1969, p. 201):

"That the error-choice method of attitude testing, apparently quite effective, has not been widely adopted is reputedly due mainly to subjects' post-test ire upon learning of the nature of the test."

QUESTIONS

1. Propose indirect techniques for assessing attitudes toward: a political candidate, a particular brand of soap, ex mental patients, marijuana, and population control.

2. The indirect techniques were included in the index measurement section of this book. Can you conceive of an indirect technique that might be classified as representational measurement? (*Hint:* try combining physiological responses with the social distance concept.)

3. Suppose you were to replicate the Hess, Seltzer, and Shlien (1965) studies by looking at pupil dilation of five heterosexual male college students and five overtly homosexual ones when viewing pictures of nude men and women. Suppose also that the results were striking in that all the heterosexual males dilated more to pictures of nude women, whereas four of the five homosexual males dilated more to pictures of nude men. (In fact, these were the exact results of the original studies.) Do you have an ethical responsibility to inform the fifth homosexual male that he may be more interested in women than he believes himself to be?

4. Imagine that you have taken a course in modern American history and that halfway through that course you were required to write an essay outlining the radical movements of this period. Imagine, also, that you were asked certain multiple-choice questions about radicals on the final exam of this course. Suppose now that you discover that the point of the essay was to allow the instructor's psychologist friend to evaluate your attitudes toward political radicalism, and that the teacher had made an effort to change your attitude toward radicalism during the last half of the semester without your knowledge; the attitude change had been assessed by the error-choice technique of the final exam. (So, of course, none of the questions concerning radicals had a correct answer.) How would you feel? How would you feel if you later discovered that your teacher and his psychologist friend had won an award for this pioneering work on attitude change?

X

Individual Differences in Attitudes as Assessed by Statement Endorsements

10.1 Introduction

One general type of index measurement technique is so common that it is treated here in a separate chapter. It is the type in which people are assessed, and the assessment is made on the basis of their agreement or disagreement with attitude statements. Basically, this type of technique is a rating scale method, because people are asked to choose one of two categories: yes, no; agree, disagree; true, false; prefer alternative A, prefer alternative B; and so on.

Such responses *could* result in a true representational measurement of the type discussed in Chapters V and VI. The endorsements and statements would have to be represented simultaneously in such a way that constraints are placed on possible endorsement patterns (e.g., as in a Guttman scale). Contexts in which statement endorsements can lead to such measurement have already been discussed in these previous chapters; the present chapter will present only techniques in which such endorsements do not yield representational measures.

The object of assessment is the person endorsing, or failing to endorse, the statement. In order to make such an assessment, it is necessary to have some prior idea about the opinion embodied in the statement—or about the sorts of people who accept or reject it. Thus, the type of assessment discussed in this chapter generally takes place in two steps; the first step involves assessing the statement, and the second involves presenting the subject with the statement to either endorse or reject. (Notice the contrast with the techniques discussed in Chapters V and VI, in which people and stimuli were assessed *simultaneously*.) This chapter is organized in terms of whether the statement itself is originally assessed by an analysis of its content or by an analysis of the characteristics of people who endorse or reject it.

10.2 Statements Assessed on the Basis of Their Content

When Thurstone developed the categorical judgment technique (see Chapter VIII, Section 8.5) he hoped that he could scale attitude statements by this method and then characterize people's attitudes by asking them to endorse or reject these statements. For example, Thurstone and Chave (1929) asked a group of "unselected" subjects to make categorical judgments about statements expressing attitudes toward "the church." These categorical judgments yield numbers meant to indicate the judged favorability of each statement—in the manner discussed in Chapter VIII, Section 8.5. Thurstone and Chave argued that the attitude toward the church of someone asked to accept or reject the scale statements could be characterized by the numbers associated with those statements endorsed; an individual's "overall" attitude toward the church might be characterized by the average number, his "range of acceptance" might be characterized by the range of the numbers, and so on. The statements investigated by Thurstone and Chave are presented in Table 1. The numbers listed to their left are their scale values according to the categorical judgment procedure. The scale values for the stimuli range from 0.2 ("I believe the church is the greatest institution in America today") to 11.0 ("I think the church is a parasite on society"). (In the Thurstone categorical judgment technique, the choice of which end of the scale is called 0 and which end is 11 is arbitrary; perhaps Thurstone's choice provided a good indirect assessment of his own attitude toward the church.)

As was discussed in Section 8.5, the choice of *who* evaluates the statements may partially determine the scale values. Despite this complication, however, the Thurstone and Chave procedure of asking some judges to evaluate the content of attitude statements in order to achieve a later evaluation of other people endorsing or rejecting these statements has become quite common. Moreover, the prior evaluation need not be made with the use of a standard technique such as Thurstone's categorical judgment method. Such prior evaluation may be made on the basis of experts' opinions about the attitude conveyed by the statement—or even on the basis of amateurs' opinions.

10.3 Statements Assessed on the Basis of the Characteristics of People Who Endorse or Reject Them

One standard procedure is to have people with known attitudes endorse or reject the statements, and then to characterize the statements in terms of how these people respond. The most common variant of this procedure is to choose two or more *criterion groups* of people with conflicting attitudes and to note the proportion of people in each group who endorse each statement. The proportion of people in a given group who endorse a given statement is taken as an estimate

Table 1   (Adapted from Thurstone & Chave, 1929)

3.3	1.	I enjoy my church because there is a spirit of friendliness there.
5.1	2.	I like the ceremonies of my church but do not miss them much when I stay away.
8.8	3.	I respect any church-member's beliefs but I think it is all "bunk."
6.1	4.	I feel the need for religion but do not find what I want in any one church.
8.3	5.	I think the teaching of the church is altogether too superficial to have much social significance.
11.0	6.	I think the church is a parasite on society.
6.7	7.	I believe in sincerity and goodness without any church ceremonies.
3.1	8.	I do not understand the dogmas or creeds of the church but I find that the church helps me to be more honest and creditable.
9.6	9.	I think the church is a hindrance to religion for it still depends upon magic, superstition, and myth.
9.2	10.	I think the church seeks to impose a lot of worn-out dogmas and medieval superstitions.
4.0	11.	When I go to church I enjoy a fine ritual service with good music.
0.8	12.	I feel the church perpetuates the values which man puts highest in his philosophy of life.
5.6	13.	Sometimes I feel that the church and religion are necessary and sometimes I doubt it.
7.5	14.	I think too much money is being spent on the church for the benefit that is being derived.
10.7	15.	I think the organized church is an enemy of science and truth.
2.2	16.	I like to go to church for I get something worthwhile to think about and it keeps my mind filled with right thoughts.
1.2	17.	I believe the church is a powerful agency for promoting both individual and social righteousness.
7.2	18.	I believe the churches are too much divided by factions and denominations to be a strong force for righteousness.
4.5	19.	I believe in what the church teaches but with mental reservations.
0.2	20.	I believe the church is the greatest institution in America today.
4.7	21.	I am careless about religion and church relationships but I would not like to see my attitude become general.
10.4	22.	The church represents shallowness, hypocrisy, and prejudice.
1.7	23.	I feel the church services give me inspiration and help me to live up to my best during the following week.
2.6	24.	I think the church keeps business and politics up to a higher standard than they would otherwise tend to maintain.

of the probability that someone picked at random from that group will endorse the statement. Furthermore, this conditional probability is assumed to be more-or-less constant for all subjects holding the attitude characterizing that group.

For example, a group of white civil rights workers may be sampled and asked whether they endorse the statement, "Blacks are essentially the same as whites." The proportion of sampled workers who endorse this statement is regarded as an estimate of the probability that white civil rights workers in general will endorse the statement, which in turn is taken as an estimate of the probability that white people in general who are favorable toward civil rights will endorse the statement. This proportion may, in turn, be contrasted with the proportion of a sampled group of Ku Klux Klan members who endorse the statement. And since these two proportions will be quite radically different, the statement will then be regarded as one that differentiates between white people who have favorable attitudes toward civil rights and those who have unfavorable attitudes. Notice that there are two very strong assumptions in this procedure. The first is that the group members actually sampled are representative of the group, and the second is that other people holding the attitudes characterizing the group will respond in a manner similar to the people in the group. For example, if a study uses members of a fraternity that excludes blacks as a criterion group of prejudiced people, it must first be assumed that those members willing to participate in the study are representative of all the fraternity members and second that the fraternity members are representative of prejudiced people. (Of course, *logically* it is only necessary to make one assumption—that the members sampled are representative of prejudiced people. But the validity of this single assumption usually depends on the validity of the other two.)

Simple as this criterion group procedure for characterizing items may appear to be, it is fraught with problems. In addition to the questionable validity of the two assumptions mentioned above, it must be kept in mind that the probability of endorsing a statement given one has a particular attitude is *not equivalent* to the probability of having that attitude given one endorses the statement. These two probabilities are technically termed the *inverses* of each other. (In order to attempt an intuitive grasp of inverse probabilities, the reader should compare the probability of being a smoker given one is a lung cancer victim—which is quite high—with the probability of getting lung cancer given one is a smoker—which is quite low, even though smokers are much more likely to get lung cancer than are nonsmokers.[1] Inverse probabilities are generally not equivalent. A fuller discussion of the relationship between inverse probabilities may be found in Meehl and Rosen (1955) or Dawes (1962).)

Despite the complications described above, the procedure of selecting attitude statements on the basis of endorsement frequencies of groups with known opposing attitudes and then maintaining that endorsement or rejection of these statements differentiates between people holding these attitudes is quite common. Often, an additional step is made: scales are constructed from a

---

[1] In addition to the lung cancer-cigarette smoking example, the reader can think of the relationship between having an advanced degree and being a lawyer; virtually all lawyers have advanced degrees, but very few of the people who have advanced degrees are lawyers; or, think of the relationship between smoking marijuana and becoming a heroin addict, or between drinking water and smoking marijuana; the belief that marijuana is a "kicker" because most heroin addicts have smoked it illustrates that the nature of inverse probabilities is not very well understood by the population at large, or perhaps is consciously or unconsciously distorted to fit preconceptions.

number of such statements, and then the number of endorsements or rejections a subject makes in common with one or another group is assumed to indicate the *degree* with which his attitude corresponds to the attitude of the group. This assumption can also be challenged on logical grounds. Why should the number of endorsements or rejections an indivudal makes that are more typical of Ku Klux Klan members than civil rights workers indicate his *degree* of racial prejudice?[2] The answer to this question is usually not based on logical or statistical considerations but instead on psychologists' experience that attitude scales constructed in this way seem to work.

Another method of characterizing attitude statements in terms of the characteristics of people who endorse or reject them is based on the idea that statements endorsed or rejected by the same people express similar attitudes. Hence, attitude statements are grouped in terms of *similarity of endorsement patterns*. Such grouping may be accomplished by factor analytic methods (see Chapter IV, Section 4.4) or by a number of other statistical clustering procedures, or even by the subjective judgment of the psychologist looking at the endorsement patterns. Once the statements are grouped, some judgment must be made about the attitudes being expressed by each group; this judgment may be based either on the content of the statements or on the type of criterion group analysis described above.

One problem with the grouping procedures for statement assessment described by Loevinger (1954) is what she terms the *attenuation paradox*. To understand this paradox, consider the extreme case of statements that have identical endorsement patterns. Clearly, two such statements would (and should) be grouped together, but the responses to the second statement do not yield any information in addition to that yielded by the responses to the first statement. The problem is general. If the endorsement patterns of two statements are *too* similar, then observing whether a subject endorses or rejects the second statement yields very little information over and above that conveyed by the observation of his response to the first. If, on the other hand, the endorsement patterns to the statements are too dissimilar, then the logic of assessing items in terms of endorsement patterns leads to the conclusion that the statements are concerned with two different attitudes, in which case we obtain no information about the type of attitude evaluated by the first statement when we observe the subjects' responses to the second. This paradox has never been fully resolved. Somewhere, clearly, there is an optimal degree to which endorsement patterns should be similar in order to select statements that are evaluating similar attitudes, but which are not too redundant. But where is this optimum?

The assessment of attitude statements on the basis of criterion group endorsements and on the basis of similarity of endorsement patterns are often termed *external* and *internal* assessment, respectively. External assessment refers to the relationship between the statement and attitude as evaluated independent-

---

[2] Logically, it could in concert with other information indicate the relative likelihood that he is a civil rights worker or member of the Ku Klux Klan. But why "degree" of prejudice?

ly of the statement (e.g., criterion group attitude is assessed without noting whether the group members endorse or reject the statement). Internal assessment is based on the relationship between statement endorsement patterns. Often, as will be demonstrated in the next section, these two general types of assessment procedures are combined.

Finally, it should be noted that even though the assessment of attitude statements on the basis of endorsement patterns *could* be done without any consideration of statement content, there must be an initial choice of statements to be so assessed. That choice is often made on the basis of statement content. The psychologist who wishes to assess a given statement by either an external or an internal assessment procedure must have some reason for believing that the statement expresses a certain attitude. This reason may be based on his own informal assessment of the statement or on a much more formal assessment—such as ratings of the statement collected by people in general, or by experts.

10.4 An Example: Verbal Racial Attitudes

Woodmansee and Cook (1967) have conducted an extensive series of investigations of verbal racial attitudes. These investigations, based on both internal and external assessment procedures, have yielded 10 sets of attitude statements. Each of these sets is meant to assess a different dimension of verbal prejudice on the part of the subjects endorsing or rejecting the statements; although these 10 different dimensions are sometimes intercorrelated, they are nevertheless distinct. These 10 sets of statements were evaluated on the basis of 4 separate studies, which will be described here in the chronological order in which they were conducted.

Study 1

The authors investigated 120 statements from past research that were thought to assess the attitude of white people toward Negroes. These statements were presented to a sample of 593 white college students, who were asked to endorse or reject each item. These students were selected

". . . from three geographical areas: Northeast, Midwest, and Border South. They were selected so as to represent a wide range of racial attitudes. One hundred fifty-nine came from prointegration organizations, while 192 belonged to anti-Negro groups: right-wing political clubs or racially exclusive fraternities or sororities. Another 242 were recruited from classes, through advertisements in college newspapers, and through announcements in college dormitories" (Woodmansee & Cook, 1967, p. 241).

The statement endorsements were subjected to a factor analysis, which resulted in 51 statements being chosen for further investigation and 69 being discarded.

Study 2

From diverse literature sources, 42 new statements were added to the 51 retained on the basis of Study 1; 609 white college students were asked to endorse or reject each statement. These students came

". . . from two geographical regions, the Midwest and the Border South. Most were tested in or recruited through large introductory college courses such as engineering orientation, English, and psychology. A representation of strong anti-Negro opinion was assured by recruiting through two southern fraternities which had openly opposed integration (N = 56)" (1967, p. 242).

A modified form of factor analysis revealed that there were 7 main dimensions (factors) underlying the endorsement patterns of these subjects.

Study 3

New Statements were added to the pool used in Study 2: these statements were meant to characterize three additional dimensions of verbal prejudice that did not appear in the results from the earlier studies. There were 317 subjects in this study who

". . . were persons whose attitude toward Negroes was unknown. Of these, 107 were from a school in a southern city and were solicited by means of newspaper ads for subjects offering money for participation in 2 hours of 'opinion testing.' The remaining 210 subjects were unpaid volunteers from introductory psychology at the University of Colorado" (1967, p. 243).

The form of modified factor analysis used in Study 2 revealed the hoped-for 10 dimensions of verbal prejudice. These dimensions are listed in Table 2 (adapted from Woodmansee & Cook, 1967, pp. 244-245), together with a single statement typical of each.

The authors constructed a questionnaire consisting of 100 statements, 10 sets of 10 meant to assess each dimension. The 10 statements in each set were chosen partially on the basis of the analyses described above and partially on the basis of controlling for response bias—that is, for 5 items in each set prejudice was indicated by endorsement, and for 5 prejudice was indicated by rejection. Each subject in this study received a score from 1 to 10 on the basis of the number of statements in each set to which he responded in a prejudiced manner. The intercorrelations between these scores are presented in Table 3 (adapted from Woodmansee & Cook, 1967, p. 244).[3]

---

[3] Notice that all the item subgroups intercorrelate quite highly with each other, *with the exception of subgroup D.*

Table 2

A.	Integration-segregation policy:	"The Negro should be afforded equal rights through integration."
B.	Acceptance in close personal relationships:	"I would not take a Negro to eat with me in a restaurant where I was well known."
C.	Negro inferiority:	"Many Negroes should receive a better education than they are now getting, but the emphasis should be on training them for jobs rather than preparing them for college."
D.	Negro superiority:	"I think that the Negroes have a kind of quiet courage which few whites have."
E.	Ease in interracial contacts:	"I would probably feel somewhat self-conscious dancing with a Negro in a public place."
F.	Derogatory beliefs:	"Although social equality of the races may be the democratic way, a good many Negroes are not yet ready to practice the self-control that goes with it."
G.	Local autonomy:	"Even though we all adopt racial integration sooner or later, the people of each community should be allowed to decide when they are ready for it."
H.	Private rights:	"A hotel owner ought to have the right to decide for himself whether he is going to rent rooms to Negro guests."
I.	Acceptance in status-superior relationships:	"If I were being interviewed for a job, I would not mind at all being evaluated by a Negro Personnel director."
J.	Gradualism:	"Gradual desegregation is a mistake because it just gives people a chance to cause further delay."

Table 3   Item Subgroup Intercorrelations and Internal Consistencies[a]

Item subgroup	A	B	C	D	E	F	G	H	I	J
A. Integration-segregation policy										
B. Acceptance in close personal relationships	.66									
C. Negro inferiority	.58	.55								
D. Negro superiority	.03	.07	.03							
E. Ease in interracial contacts	.27	.47	.27	.20						
F. Derogatory beliefs	.49	.52	.54	.20	.41					
G. Local autonomy	.60	.51	.43	.20	.32	.56				
H. Private rights	.47	.46	.39	.26	.36	.53	.74			
I. Acceptance in status-superior relationships	.69	.69	.63	-.02	.30	.47	.39	.38		
J. Gradualism	.29	.36	.27	.23	.40	.52	.66	.60	.22	

[a]$N = 317$

Study 4

The 100-statement questionnaire was administered to 313 subjects who (1967, p. 243):

"... were chosen for their participation in groups which might be expected to have a majority of members holding specified attitudes toward Negroes. We regarded these subjects as criterion groups against which to assess the validity of our attitude dimensions. The groups and the assumptions about their members' attitudes are listed below:

"Group I. Subjects assumed to have strongly equalitarian attitudes and to be actively concerned with race relations (e.g., CORE, NAACP, race-relations councils).

"Group II. Subjects assumed to have equalitarian attitudes but not the active concern of Group I. Students who voluntarily expose themselves to attitude-related issues in elective race-relations classes fit this description.

"Group III. Subjects assumed to have somewhat anti-Negro attitudes but not to be actively concerned with questions of race relations. Groups having a high proportion of members of this type are hard to identify. An earlier study ... found a higher proportion of moderately or extremely anti-Negro subjects in right-wing political organizations than in other student groups; therefore, subjects for Group III were recruited from these organizations (e.g., Young Americans for Freedom).

"Group IV. Subjects assumed to be anti-Negro and to be actively concerned with race relations. Social fraternity groups which had recently gone on record on their campuses as being opposed to inclusion of Negroes in their membership were solicited as respondents in this study. All of these subjects were paid for their participation in the study."

Each subject in this study, as in the previous study, was given a score of 1 to 10 on each dimension depending on his endorsement or rejection of the items. The subject's endorsement or rejection of each item was scored +1 if he responded in an *unprejudiced* manner and 0 if he responded in a prejudiced one. The average scores for each of these groups on each of these dimensions are presented in Table 4 (Table 2 of Woodmansee & Cook, 1967, p. 247), along with other statistical information concerning the difference between these scores.

It appears that the *group* scores correspond very well with what we would expect on the basis of the group composition.

Although the authors refer to these results as constituting criterion group validation of their attitude scales, it should be pointed out that not all the members of each group can be expected to share the same attitude. Perhaps none of the members of Group I were antiblack, but surely Groups II to IV may have contained both prejudiced and unprejudiced members. (For example, it is

Table 4   Analyses of Variance of Subscale Scores of Criterion Group Subjects, by Region

Subscale	Criterion Level	Western[a]			Border South[b]		
		$\bar{X}$[c]	SD	F	$\bar{X}$	SD	F
Integration-segregation policy	I	9.82	0.39		9.80	0.72	
	II	9.49	1.46		7.92	2.84	
	III	6.46	3.60		4.00	2.94	
	IV	7.41	2.79		5.11	3.40	
				17.85[e]			33.72[e]
Acceptance in close personal	I	9.73	0.46		9.49	1.09	
relationships	II	8.37	2.85		5.00	3.82	
	III	6.49	3.71		3.26	2.88	
	IV	6.15	2.87		2.39	2.76	
				11.19[e]			49.98[e]
Negro inferiority	I	9.18	1.01		8.97	1.15	
	II	8.47	1.48		7.56	2.12	
	III	6.83	2.67		5.66	2.17	
	IV	6.76	2.12		5.02	2.82	
				14.07[e]			24.90[e]
Negro superiority	I	3.00	2.35		3.29	3.27	
	II	1.60	2.12		2.88	2.88	
	III	1.29	1.30		1.53	1.70	
	IV	2.11	1.72		1.16	1.55	
				4.35[d]			6.89[e]
Ease in interracial contacts	I	7.18	1.92		4.91	2.64	
	II	2.54	2.20		1.76	2.09	
	III	1.77	1.50		1.29	1.31	
	IV	1.43	1.15		1.23	1.67	
				56.67[e]			29.41[e]
Derogatory beliefs	I	7.18	1.37		7.03	1.84	
	II	5.41	2.30		4.28	2.09	
	III	3.00	2.00		1.66	1.66	
	IV	2.89	1.83		2.18	1.54	
				33.75[e]			70.85[e]
Local autonomy	I	9.32	0.84		8.89	1.64	
	II	7.04	3.09		6.08	3.59	
	III	2.89	2.88		2.42	1.97	
	IV	4.89	2.90		2.43	2.38	
				30.12			63.34
Private rights	I	8.68	0.99		7.97	1.85	
	II	5.99	3.52		4.12	3.24	
	III	0.83	1.36		1.63	2.14	
	IV	3.17	3.00		1.05	1.71	
				45.17[e]			76.63[e]
Acceptance in status-superior	I	9.96	0.21		9.80	0.53	
relationships	II	9.15	1.66		7.96	2.49	
	III	7.60	3.26		5.63	3.20	
	IV	7.63	2.52		5.09	3.41	

Table 4   Analyses of Variance of Subscale Scores of Criterion Group Subjects, by Region

				9.25^e			23.40^e
Gradualism	I	7.45	2.86		7.00	2.62	
	II	4.32	3.38		3.36	3.53	
	III	1.00	1.46		1.18	1.72	
	IV	2.39	2.41		1.00	1.48	
				29.13^e			53.90^e

[a] N for each criterion level: I = 22, II = 68, III = 35, IV = 46; and df = 3,167 for all western region analyses.

[b] N for each criterion level: I = 35, II = 25, III = 38, IV = 44; and df = 3,138 for all Border South analyses.

[c] The greater the mean score the more equalitarian the attitude.

[d] $p < .01$.

[e] $p < .001$.

possible, especially considering the year that this study was conducted, that some members of fraternities excluding blacks were not themselves antiblack.) And, in fact, the authors characterize Group III as consisting of a mixture of people with different attitudes. Hence, the validation procedure might better be characterized as one based on *mixed* groups (for a discussion of such validation, see Dawes & Meehl, 1966).

10.5 Relationship to Personality Inventory Scales

The methods described in Sections 10.2 and 10.3 for selecting attitude statements to evaluate individual differences in attitude are basically the same as those used for selection of personality inventory items to evaluate individual differences in personality traits. Such methods are reviewed by Goldberg and Hase (1967) and Hase and Goldberg (1967). These authors distinguish between intuitive, internal, and external strategies for selecting items to evaluate each trait; their "intuitive" strategy is basically the same as that discussed in Section 10.2, although their internal and external strategies include the methods discussed in Section 10.3—as well as other methods. It should not be surprising that the methods described in this chapter are the same as those for choosing items for personality questionnaires. Attitudes, as assessed by the endorsement method discussed in this chapter, can properly be regarded as personality traits.

QUESTIONS

1. Suppose that you wished to distinguish attitudes toward aging from attitudes toward other natural biological phenomena (e.g., sex). Suppose that a friend wished to evaluate individual differences in attitude toward aging. What different types of techniques would you and your friend use? How would you differ in the way(s) in which you constructed your techniques?
2. Thurstone and Chave used a rating scale technique to characterize the content of their statements concerning the church; they could, in contrast, have used a comparative judgment technique, or one of the other magnitude techniques described in Chapter III. Could a proximity technique (Chapter IV) be used to characterize statement content? Could factor analysis? If so, how might these techniques be employed, and how would we characterize people who endorse or reject statements assessed by these techniques?
3. Two statements are highly correlated if there are many endorse-endorse and reject-reject responses to them and very few endorse-reject and reject-endorse responses. What is the correlational pattern of statements forming a Guttman scale? Are they necessarily highly correlated? Can they be negatively correlated?
4. Contrast grouping attitude statements together on the basis of similar endorsement patterns with arranging them on a Guttman scale on the basis of such patterns. What is the essential difference between the former procedure (an index measurement technique) and the latter (a representational measurement technique)?
5. Suppose that you constructed statements that appeared to assert radical or conservative attitudes. Suppose, also, you obtained endorsement patterns of a group of SDS members and a group of YAF (Young Americans for Freedom) members and found no differences between the groups. What would you conclude?
6. Both the statements "I am being followed" and "I like mechanics magazines" tend to be endorsed more by people classified as "paranoid" than by people classified as "normal." The content of the former statements leads to the expectation that paranoids will more often say "yes" than will normals, but the content of the latter does not. (Of course, it may be possible after the fact to make up a rationale for the greater endorsement frequency of the second item on the part of paranoids, but it might also be possible to make up a rationale for greater endorsement frequency of the item "I do not like mechanics magazines.") Suppose a statement that apparently had nothing to do with racial attitude distinguished between groups of prejudiced and groups of nonprejudiced individuals. Would it be proper to call such a statement an "attitude statement"? Could it form part of an "attitude scale"? (For example, one good candidate for such a statement is "I think Lincoln was a greater President than Washington." In fact, this statement differentiates almost perfectly between southern whites and blacks.)

7. Suppose that someone was deeply involved in an issue—for example, either extremely anti-Communist, or extremely opposed to anti-Communism as a philosophy. Suppose, also, that this person were to make up attitude statements to differentiate between groups who are on different sides of this issue. On the basis of the material in Chapter IX, what might be expected to happen when the questions are presented to the two groups for endorsement?

Conclusion

The following chapter discusses the relationship between representational measurement and index measurement; in addition, it discusses the relationship between structure in attitude and the possibility of measuring it.

XI

Structure in Attitude

"The search for structure is inherent in behavior" (Garner, 1962, p. 339).

11.1 Similarities Between Representational Measurement and Index Measurement

Both are based on valid prediction. Representational measurement leads to prediction of the behavior of a well-defined empirical relational system, while index measurement is useful only insofar as it predicts—future behavior, representational measures, or other index measurement results. (See Chapter VIII, Section 8.5.) Even the psychological justification for rating scales (Chapter VIII, Section 8.7) is ultimately based on prediction—for example, of the experimenters' or subjects' subjective impressions of compatibility, or of interpretable experimental results.

Generally, the rationale presented in this book for representational techniques is that their predictions are precise, whereas that presented for index measurement techniques is that their predictions are useful. But our representational techniques should also be useful, and the more precise the predictions of index measurement techniques, the more valuable they will be.

11.2 The Basic Difference Between Representational Measurement and Index Measurement

Is the difference, then, mainly one of degree? in that the predictions derived from representational measurement merely are more precise than those derived from index measurement? The answer proposed here to this question is a tentative "no." A distinction can be drawn between the well-defined empirical relational system that a representational measurement technique represents and the loosely-defined domain about which the index measurement technique yields predictions. Of course, there is a probabilistic element in the predictions of both types of techniques. But, when a representational measurement tech-

146

nique fails to make perfect predictions about our observations, we attribute the lack of perfection to the fact that our observations do not perfectly correspond to the system itself (see Section 7.2 for Coombs' distinction between observations and data). Lack of precision of predictions from index measurement techniques, in contrast, is attributed to lack of perfect correspondence between the assessments made by the technique and the behavior in the domain it assesses. Thus, there must be a perfect correspondence between an object's weight and its behavior in an idealized pan balance, or between a subject's response to an item requiring only arithmetic ability and his level of such ability; where discrepancies are found, they are attributed to the fact that the pan balance we actually observe may not be ideal, or the item we have selected may not be one that measures only arithmetic ability. On the other hand, there need not be a perfect correspondence between the way in which a man responds to a rating scale assessing his attitude toward the President and the way in which he votes—even if the rating scale is an ideally good one.

Coombs (personal communication) believes that this distinction can be understood by drawing an analogy to the distinction between science and engineering. "As scientists we are interested in the laws of behavior and in building a system to test whether certain axioms [conditions] are true or what the domain is for which the axioms are true." That is, as scientists we are interested in the nature of empirical relational systems and their scope. Representational measurement yields insight into such systems. As engineers we are interested in things that work; index measures can work. Moreover, just as scientific discoveries can lead to engineering advances, representational measures can be useful. And just as it is possible to achieve engineering accomplishments in the absence of a set of well-specified scientific principles, index measures can be highly predictive. Finally, just as engineering advances can result in scientific insight, the predictive success of a particular index measure may lead to the discovery of a true empirical relational system.

11.3 The Problem Is Empirical

Measurement of attitude is a joint function of the behavior of the attitudes being assessed and the system proposed by the investigator to assess them. Representational measurement involves two conditions: the attitudinal behavior must be systematic enough that an empirical relational system may be identified, and the person who wishes to measure this behavior must know of, or invent, an appropriate numerical system for representing this behavior. If, on the other hand, the investigator wishes to construct an index measurement technique, then he must show that it indeed has some usefulness. In either case, the question of whether attitude measurement is possible cannot be settled by philosophical debate, or meta-scientific predisposition.

Thus, it is futile to argue either that attitudes *must* be measured before they can be studied scientifically or that human attitudes are so "complex" or "personal" or whatever that they cannot be measured. Both arguments are based on a misunderstanding of the nature of measurement.

The argument that attitudes must be measured before they can be studied scientifically stems from the belief that they can be measured simply because they exist. This belief is expressed in F. L. Thorndike's famous dictum: "Whatever exists, exists in some quantity; whatever exists in quantity can be measured" (see Chapter II, question 5). As pointed out in Chapter II (Section 2.1), although it is true that things exist, it is not things that are measured; instead, the *attributes* of things are measured. (When we measure the weight of an object, we do not measure the object; we measure its weight.) Moreover, the attributes are measured not by some sort of apprehension of the existential glop of which things are composed, but rather by the behavior of the things.

The argument that attitudes cannot be measured because of their intrinsic characteristics likewise rests on a misconception. If an empirical relational system exists, and if an investigator is clever enough to discover or invent a numerical representation of this system, then measurement has in fact occurred. Or if the investigator is able to develop an index measurement technique that leads to predictions that are found to be correct, then index measurement has occurred. The question of whether the investigator is capable of doing either of these things is a purely empirical question. There is no such thing as "misquantification," or "premature quantification." (In fact, it can be argued that there is no such thing as "quantification." One does not observe a phenomenon and then "quantify" it; instead, the phenomenon must behave in certain predictable ways, and the investigator must choose a measurement system that reflects this behavior.)

11.4 Structure

Structure exists whenever all logical possibilities are not equally likely. Empirical relational systems are structured. For example, in the situation where object *a* outweighs object *b* and object *b* outweighs object *c,* there are two logical possibilities concerning the relationship between *a* and *c—a* may outweigh *c,* or *c* may outweigh *a;* in point of fact, the first possibility always occurs and the second never occurs. Or when crime *a* is said to be more serious than crime *b* by 61 percent of the population and crime *b* is said to be more serious than crime *c* by 67 percent of the population, it is logically possible for any percentage of the population from 0 to 100 to say that a crime *a* is more serious than crime *c;* if the Thurstone comparative judgment technique accurately represents such judgments, then the obtained proportion must be close to 77 percent. If a subject says that occupation *a* is twice as prestigeful as occupation *b,* and he says that *b* is twice as prestigeful as *c,* he is perfectly free to choose any number to indicate his feelings about the ratio of prestige of *a* to *c;* if a numerical ratio scale accurately represents his judgments, then he must choose the ratio 4 to 1. If subject No. 1 passes item *a* but flunks *b*, it is logically conceivable that subject No. 2 passes *b* and flunks *a*, or passes both, or fails both; if, however, subjects and items are represented by the interlocking order of a Guttman scale, then the probability of subject No. 2 passing *b* but flunking *a* should be zero (or near zero). The reader may for himself look at each of the other examples of representational attitude measurement and determine how it is that such measurement can occur only if a very small proportion of subjects' *possible* responses to stimuli in fact occur. Representational measurement is possible because the empirical relational system represented is structured.

In addition, index measurement is possible only if there is structure. For example, consider the semantic differential technique (Chapter VIII, Section 8.2). This technique is based on the fact that ratings on a great many semantic scales may be fairly well predicted from ratings on the hypothetical factors of evaluation, potency, and activity. Logically, when an individual rates a concept, his rating of the concept on scale *a* could be paired with any rating on scale *b;* if, however, all such pairings are equally likely, then there would be no way of predicting the ratings from the three hypothetical factors. It is because all such pairings are *not* equally likely, because the ratings on the scales are correlated, that it was possible for Osgood and his colleagues to perform the factor analysis and discover the three hypothetical factors. (If all pairs of ratings were equally likely, the correlation between all pairs of semantic scales would be zero, and a factor analysis would yield as many factors as scales.) Or consider the empirical justification of rating scale methods; again, it is logically possible for any rating scale response to be paired with any sort of behavior; as pointed out in the first section of Chapter VIII, there is no logical reason why the person who says he is delighted with the policies of his President may not decide to shoot him the next day. The rating scale is useful only because people who respond to it differently are not equally likely to behave in the same ways. That is, there is *structure* in people's categorical responses and their behaviors.

Moreover, the existence of structure is not independent of the possibility of measurement. Since structure is a prerequisite to measurement, measurement can exist only in situations in which structure exists. Equivalently, the success of measurement implies the existence of structure. As our understanding of structure in attitude increases, our ability to measure it will also; as our ability to measure increases, so will our understanding of this structure.

References

Abelson, R. P. A technique and a model for multidimensional attitude scaling. *Public Opinion Quarterly*, 1954, **18**, 405-418.

Abelson, R. P. Computers, polls, & public opinion—some puzzles & paradoxes. *Trans-action*, 1968, **5**, 20-27.

Adams, E. W. On the nature and purpose of measurement. *Synthese*, 1966, **16**, 125-169.

Adams, E. W., Fagot, R. F., & Robinson, R. E. A theory of appropriate statistics. *Psychometrika*, 1965, **30**, 99-127.

Adorno, T. W., Frenkel-Brunswik, E., Levinson, D. J., & Sanford, R. N. *The authoritarian personality*. New York: Harper, 1950.

Ager, J. W., & Dawes, R. M. The effect of judges' attitudes on judgment. *Journal of Personality and Social Psychology*, 1965, **1**, 533-538.

Allport, G. W. Attitudes. In C. Murchison (Ed.), *Handbook of social psychology*. Worcester, Mass.: Clark University Press, 1935.

Anderson, N. H. Scales and statistics: Parametric and nonparametric. *Psychological Bulletin*, 1961, **58**, 305-316.

Anderson, N. H. Averaging versus adding as a stimulus-combination rule in impression formation. *Journal of Experimental Psychology*. 1965, **70**, 394-400.

Anderson, N. H. Averaging model analysis of set size effect on impression formation. *Journal of Experimental Psychology*, 1967, **75**, 158-165.

Anderson, N. H. Functional measurement and psychophysical judgment. *Psychological Review*, 1970, **77**, 153-170.

Anderson, N. H. Integration theory and attitude change. *Psychological Review*, 1971, **78**, 171-206.

Atwood, R. W., & Howell, R. J. Pupillometric and personality test score differences of female aggressing pedophiliacs and normals. *Psychonomic Science*, 1971, **22**, 115-116.

Beals, R., Krantz, D. H., & Tversky, A. Foundations of multidimensional scaling. *Psychological Review*, 1968, **75**, 127-142.

Bennett, J. F. Determination of the number of independent parameters of a score matrix from the examination of rank orders. *Psychometrika*, 1956, **21**, 383-393.

Bogardus, E. S. Measuring social distances. *Journal of Applied Sociology*, 1925, **9**, 299-308.

Bogardus, E. S. *Immigration and race attitudes*. Boston: Heath, 1928.

Braatz, G. A. Preference intransitivity as an indicator of cognitive slippage in schizophrenia. *Journal of Abnormal Psychology*, 1970, **75**, 1-6.

Bumpass, L. L., & Westoff, C. F. *The later years of childbearing*. Princeton, N.J.: Princeton Universtiy Press, 1970.

Campbell, D. T. The indirect assessment of social attitudes. *Psychological Bulletin*, 1950, **47**, 15-38.

Campbell, D. T., & Fiske, D. W. Convergent and discriminant validation by the multitrait-multimethod matrix. *Psychological Bulletin*, 1959, **56**, 81-105.

151

Campbell, D. T., & Stanley, J. C. Experimental and quasi-experimental designs for research on teaching. In N. L. Gage (Ed.), *Handbook of research on teaching.* Chicago: Rand McNally, 1963.

Comrey, A. L. A proposed method for absolute ratio scaling. *Psychometrika,* 1950, **15**, 317-325.

Coombs, C. H. Psychological scaling without a unit of measurement. *Psychological Review,* 1950, **57**, 145-158.

Coombs, C. H. Some symmetries and dualities among measurement data matrices. In *Thurstone Hall Dedication Conference.* New York: Holt, Rinehart & Winston, 1963.

Coombs, C. H. *A theory of data.* New York: Wiley, 1964.

Coombs, C. H. Thurstone's measurement of social values revisited forty years' later. *Journal of Personality and Social Psychology,* 1967, **6**, 85-90.

Coombs, C. H., Dawes, R. M., & Tversky, A. *Mathematical psychology: An elementary introduction.* Englewood Cliffs, N.J.: Prentice-Hall, 1970.

Cooper, J. B., & Pollock, D. The identification of prejudicial attitudes by the galvanic skin response. *Journal of Social Psychology,* 1959, **50**, 241-245.

Dawes, R. M. A note on base rates and psychometric efficiency. *Journal of Consulting Psychology,* 1962, **26**, 422-424.

Dawes, R. M. Social selection based on multidimensional criteria. *Journal of Abnormal and Social Psychology,* 1964, **68**, 104-109.

Dawes, R. M. Racial preference and social choice. *Science,* 1966, 151, 1248.

Dawes, R. M. Algebraic models of cognition (summarized by E. Saraga). In *Algebraic models in psychology:* Proceedings of the NUFFIC International Summer Session in Science at "Het Oude Hof," The Hague, August 5-17, 1968. These lecture notes are available from NUFFIC through Psychological Institute of the University of Leyden, Rijnsburgerweg 169, Leyden, The Netherlands, Europe.

Dawes, R. M. Sexual heterogeneity of children as a determinant of American family size. *Oregon Research Institute Research Bulletin,* 1970, Vol. 10, No. 8.

Dawes, R. M., Brown, M. E., & Kaplan, N. The skewed hourglass: A configurational approach to constructing a Guttman scale when domination is unspecified. Paper presented at the annual convention of the Midwestern Psychological Association, Chicago, April 1965.

Dawes, R. M., & Kramer, E. A proximity analysis of vocally expressed emotion. *Perceptual and Motor Skills,* 1966, **22**, 571-574.

Dawes, R. M., & Meehl, P. E. Mixed group validation: A method for determining the validity of diagnostic signs without using criterion groups. *Psychological Bulletin,* 1966, **66**, 63-67.

Dawes, R. M., Singer, D., & Lemons, F. An experimental analysis of the contrast effect and its implications for intergroup communication and the indirect assessment of attitude. *Journal of Personality and Social Psychology.* 1972, in press. Also, *Oregon Research Institute Research Bulletin,* 1972, Vol. 11, No. 12.

Dawes, R. M., & Winter, B. B. Guttman scales. *Oregon Research Institute Technical Report,* 1969, Vol. 9, No. 1.

De Soto, C. B., London, M., & Handel, S. Social reasoning and spatial paralogic. *Journal of Personality and Social Psychology,* 1965, **2**, 513-521.

Ekman, G., & Künnapas, T. Scales of conservatism. *Perceptual and Motor Skills,* 1963, **16**, 329-334.

Fagot, R. F., & Stewart, M. R. A test of the response bias model of bisection. *Perception and Psychophysics,* 1970, **7**, 257-262.

Fairbanks, G. Recent experimental investigation of vocal pitch in voice. *Journal of the Acoustical Society of America,* 1940, **11,** 457-466.

Fairbanks, G., & Hoaglin, L. W. An experimental study of the durational characteristics of the voice during expression of emotions. *Speech Monographs,* 1941, **8,** 85-90.

Fairbanks, G., & Pronovost, W. An experimental study of the pitch characteristics of the voice during expression of emotions. *Speech Monographs,* 1939, **8,** 87-104.

Festinger L. In collaboration with V. Allen, M. Braden, L. K. Cannon, J. R. Davidson, J. D. Jecker, S. B. Kiesler, & E. Walster. *Conflict, decision and dissonance.* Stanford, California: Stanford University Press, 1964.

Fishbein, M., & Hunter, R. Summation versus balance in attitude organization and change. *Journal of Abnormal and Social Psychology,* 1964, **69,** 505-510.

Freedman, D. S., Freedman, R., & Whelpton, P. K. Size of family and preference for children of each sex. *American Journal of Sociology,* 1960, **66,** 141-146.

Galanter, E. H. An axiomatic and experimental study of sensory order and measure. *Psychological Review,* 1956, **63,** 16-28.

Garner, W. R. *Uncertainty and structure as psychological concepts.* New York: Wiley, 1962.

Gleason, T. C. A general model for nonmetric multidimensional scaling. *Michigan Mathematical Psychology Program: MMPP 67-3.* Ann Arbor, Michigan, June 1967.

Gleason, T. C. Multidimensional scaling of sociometric data. *Research Center for Group Dynamics Technical Report,* 1969.

Goldberg, D., & Coombs, C. H. Some applications of unfolding theory to fertility analysis. *Emerging techniques in population research.* Proceedings of the 1962 Annual Conference of the Milbank Memorial Fund.

Goldberg, L. R., & Hase, H. D. Strategies and tactics of personality inventory construction: An empirical investigation. *Oregon Research Institute Research Monograph,* 1967, Vol. 7, No. 1.

Goldberg, L. R., & Werts, C. E. The reliability of clinicians' judgments: A multitrait-multimethod approach. *Journal of Consulting Psychology,* 1966, **30,** 199-206.

Goodman, N. *The structure of appearance.* Cambridge: Harvard University Press, 1951.

Guttman, L. A basis for scaling qualitative data. *American Sociological Review,* 1944, **9,** 139-150.

Guttman, L. Chapters 2, 3, 6, 8, and 9 in Stouffer et al. (Eds.), *Measurement and prediction.* Princeton: Princeton University Press, 1950.

Guttman, L. A partial-order scalogram classification of projective techniques. Appearing in *Festschrift in honor of Joseph Zubin.* Wiley, 1971.

Harmond, K. R. Measuring attitudes by error-choice: An indirect method. *Journal of Abnormal and Social Psychology,* 1948, **43,** 38-48.

Hase, H. D., & Goldberg, L. R. Comparative validity of different strategies of constructing personality inventory scales. *Psychological Bulletin,* 1967, **67,** 231-248.

Hays, W. L. *Statistics for psychologists.* New York: Holt, Rinehart & Winston, 1963. P. 74.

Hays, W. L., & Bennett, J. F. Multidimensional unfolding: Determining configuration from complete rank order preference data. *Psychometrika,* 1961, **26,** 221-238.

Hess, E. H. Attitude and pupil size. *Scientific American,* 1965, **212,** 46-54.

Hess, E. H., Seltzer, A. L., & Shlien, J. M. Pupil response of hetero- and homosexual males to pictures of men and women: A pilot study. *Journal of Abnormal Psychology,* 1965, **70,** 165-168.

Hölder, O. Die Axiome der Quantität und die Lehre von Mass. *Berichte* uber die Verhandlugen der Königlich Säclisischen Gesellschaft der Wissenschaften zu Leipzig, Mathematisch-Physische Classe, 1901, **53,** 1-64.

Horst, P. *The prediction of personal adjustment.* Social Science Research Council, 1941. Pp. 251-364.

Hovland, C. I., & Sherif, M. Judgmental phenomena and scales of attitude measurement: Item displacement in Thurstone scales. *Journal of Abnormal and Social Psychology,* 1952, **47**, 822-832.

Jensen, A. R. How much can we boost IQ and scholastic achievement? *Harvard Educational Review,* 1969, **39**, 1-123.

Johnson, H. H., & Foley, J. M. Some effects of placebo and experiment conditions in research on methods of teaching. *Journal of Educational Psychology,* 1969, **60**, 6-10.

Karlins, M., Coffman, T. L., & Walters, G. On the fading of social stereotypes: Studies in three generations of college students. *Journal of Personality and Social Psychology,* 1969, **13**, 1-16.

Katz, D. The functional approach to the study of attitudes. *Public Opinion Quarterly,* 1960, **24**, 163-204.

Katz, D., & Braly, K. W. Racial stereotypes of 100 college students. *Journal of Abnormal and Social Psychology,* 1933, **28**, 280-290.

Kelly, G. A. *The psychology of personal constructs.* Vol. 1. *A theory of personality.* New York: W. W. Norton, 1955.

Kelly, H. H., Hovland, C. I., Scwartz, M., & Abelson, R. The influence of judges' attitudes in three methods of attitude scaling. *Journal of Social Psychology,* 1955, **42**, 147-158.

Kjedahl, W. O. Factors in a presidential candidate's image. Unpublished doctoral dissertation, University of Oregon, 1969.

Klahr, D. A Monte Carlo investigation of the statistical significance of Kruskal's nonmetric scaling procedure. *Psychometrika,* 1969, **34**, 319-330.

Koslin, B. L., & Pargament, R. Effects of attitude on the discrimination of opinion statements. *Journal of Experimental Social Psychology,* 1969, **5**, 245-264.

Kramer, E. The judgment of personal characteristics and emotions from non-verbal properties of voice. *Psychological Bulletin,* 1963, **60**, 408-420.

Krantz, D. H., Luce, R. D., Suppes, P., & Tversky, A. *Foundations of measurement.* New York: Academic Press, 1971.

Krantz, D. H., & Tversky, A. Conjoint-measurement analysis of composition rules in psychology. *Psychological Review,* 1971, **78**, 151-169.

Kruskal, J. B. Multidimensional scaling by optimizing goodness of fit to a nonmetric hypothesis. *Psychometrika,* 1964a, **29**, 1-27.

Kruskal, J. B. Nonmetric multidimensional scaling: A numerical method. *Psychometrika,* 1964b, **29**, 115-129.

Künnapas, T. & Wikström, I. Measurement of occupational preferences. A comparison of scaling methods. *Psychological Laboratory, University of Stockholm Report No. 156,* 1963.

Lafave, L., & Sherif, M. Reference scale and placement of items with the own categories technique. *Journal of Social Psychology,* 1968, **76**, 75-82.

LaPiere, R. T. Attitudes versus actions. *Social Forces,* 1934, **13**, 230-237.

Likert, R. A technique for the measurement of attitudes. *Archives of Psychology,* 1932, No. 140, 5-53.

Lingoes, J. C. An IBM-7090 program for Guttman-Lingoes smallest space analysis: I. *Behavioral Sciences,* 1965, **10**, 183-184.

Lingoes, J. C. Recent computational advances in nonmetric methodology for the behavioral sciences. In *Proceedings of the International Symposium: Mathematical and Computational Methods in Social Sciences,* International Computation Center, Rome, 1966, 1-38.

Lingoes, J. C. The rationale of the Guttman-Lingoes nonmetric series: A letter to Doctor Philip Runkel. *Multivariate Behavioral Research,* 1968, 3, 495-508.

Loevinger, J. The attenuation paradox in test theory. *Psychological Bulletin,* 1954, 51, 493-504.

Luce, R. D., & Tukey, J. W. Simultaneous conjoint measurement: A new type of fundamental measurement. *Journal of Mathematical Psychology,* 1964, 1, 1-27.

McGee, V. E. A multidimensional analysis of 'elastic' distances. *British Journal of Mathematical Statistical Psychology,* 1966, 19, 181-196.

Maloney, J. C. Psychology experiments without subjects' consent. *Science,* 1966, 152, 1455.

Manis, M., Gleason, T. C., & Dawes, R. M. The evaluation of complex social stimuli. *Journal of Personality and Social Psychology,* 1966, 3, 404-419.

Markle, G. E., & Nam, C. B. Sex predetermination: Its impact on fertility. *Social Biology,* 1971, 18, 73-83.

Meehl, P. E., & Rosen, A. Antecedent probability and the efficiency of psychometric signs, patterns, or cutting scores. *Psychological Bulletin,* 1955, 52, 194-216.

Melton, A. W. Some behavior characteristics of museum visitors. *Psychological Bulletin,* 1933, 30, 720-721.

Melton, A. W. Distribution of attention in galleries in a museum of science and industry. *Museum News,* 1936, 13, (3), 5-8.

Messick, S. J. The preception of social attitudes. *Journal of Abnormal and Social Psychology,* 1956, 52, 57-66.

Milgram, S., Mann, L., & Harter, S. The lost-letter technique of social research. *Public Opinion Quarterly,* 1965, 29, 437-438.

Miller, S. E. Psychology experiments without subjects' consent. *Science,* 1966, 152, 15.

Mosier, C. I. Psychophysics and mental test theory: Fundamental postulates and elementary theorems. *Psychological Review,* 1940, 47, 355-366.

Newcomb, T. M. *The acquaintance process.* New York: Holt, Rinehart & Winston, 1961.

Norman, W. T. Stability-characteristics of the semantic differential. *American Journal of Psychology,* 1959, 72, 581-584.

Orne, M. T. On the social psychology of the psychological experiment: With particular reference to demand characteristics and their implications. *American Psychologist,* 1962, 17, 776-783.

Osgood, C. E., & Luria, Z. A blind analysis of a case of multiple personality using the semantic differential. *Journal of Abnormal and Social Psychology,* 1954, 49, 579-591.

Osgood, C. E., Suci, G. J., & Tannenbaum, P. H. *The measurement of meaning.* Urbana: University of Illinois Press, 1957.

Peabody, D. Authoritarian scales and response bias. *Psychological Bulletin,* 1966, 65, 11-23.

Peabody, D. Group judgments in the Philippines: Evaluative and descriptive aspects. *Journal of Personality and Social Psychology,* 1968, 10, 290-300.

Pfanzagl, J. *Theory of measurement.* New York: Wiley, 1968.

Reich, J., & Sherif, M. Ego-involvement as a factor in attitude assessment by the own categories technique. Norman: The University of Oklahoma, 1963 (mimeographed).

Rinn, J. L. Group behavior descriptions: A nonmetric multidimensional analysis. *Journal of Abnormal and Social Psychology,* 1963, **67**, 173-176.

Robinson, J. P., Rusk, J. G., & Head, K. B. *Measures of political attitudes.* Ann Arbor: University of Michigan Institute for Social Research, 1969.

Rokeach, M. *The open and closed mind.* New York: Basic Books, 1960.

Rokeach, M., & Mezei, L. Race and shared belief as factors in social choice. *Science,* 1966, **151**, 167-172. Copyright 1966 by the American Association for the Advancement of Science.

Rorer, L. G. The great response-style myth. *Psychological Bulletin,* 1965, **63**, 129-156.

Rorer, L. G., & Goldberg, L. R. Acquiescence and the vanishing variance component. *Journal cf Applied Psychology,* 1965, **49**, 422-430.

Runkel, P. J. Cognitive similarity in facilitating communication. *Sociometry,* 1956, **19**, 178-191.

Rutherford, B., Morrison, D., & Campbell, D. T. *Measurement models for the social sciences,* 1972, in press.

Schubert, G. A psychometric model of the Supreme Court. *American Behavioral Scientist,* 1961, **5**, 14-18.

Scott, W. A. Attitude measurement. In G. Lindzey, & E. Aronson (Eds.), *The handbook of social psychology. Vol. 2.* (2nd ed.), Reading, Mass.: Addison-Wesley Publishing Co., 1968.

Selltiz, C., Edrich, H., & Cook, S. W. Ratings of favorableness of statements about a social group as an indicator of attitude toward the group. *Journal of Personality and Social Psychology,* 1965, **2**, 408-415.

Shaw, M. E., & Wright, J. M. *Scales for the measurement of attitudes.* New York: McGraw-Hill, 1967.

Shepard, R. N. The analysis of proximities: Multidimensional scaling with an unknown distance function. I. *Psychometrika,* 1962a, **27**, 125-140.

Shepard, R. N. The analysis of proximities: Multidimensional scaling with an unknown distance function. II. *Psychometrika,* 1962b, **27**, 219-246.

Shepard, R. N. Analysis of proximities as a technique for the study of information processing in man. *Human Factors,* 1963, 33-48.

Sherif, M., & Hovland, C. I. Judgmental phenomena and scales of attitude measurement: Placement of items with individual choice of number categories. *Journal of Abnormal and Social Psychology,* 1953, **48**, 135-141.

Sherif, M., & Sherif, C. W. *Social psychology.* New York: Harper & Row, 1969.

Sherif, C. W., Sherif, M., & Nebergall, R. E. *Attitude and attitude change: The social judgment-involvement approach.* Philadelphia: W. B. Saunders, 1965.

Sikes, M. P., & Cleveland, S. E. Human relations training for police and community. *American Psychologist,* 1968, **23**, 766-769.

Spaeth, H. J. Unidimensionality and item invariance in judicial scaling. *Behavioral Science,* 1965, **10**, 290-304.

Standen, A. Psychological experiments without subjects' consent. *Science,* 1966, **152**, 1455-1456.

Stevens, S. S. Mathematics, measurement, and psychophysics. In S. S. Stevens (ed.), *Handbook of experimental psychology.* New York: Wiley, 1951.

Stevens, S. S. A metric for the social consensus. *Science,* 1966, **151**, 530-541.

Stevens, S. S. Measurement, statistics, and the schemapiric view. *Science,* 1968, **161**, 849-856.

Suppes, P., & Zinnes, J. L. Basic measurement theory. In R. D. Luce, R. R. Bush, & E. Galanter (Eds.), *Handbook of mathematical psychology.* Vol. 1. New York: Wiley, 1963. Pp. 1-76.

Thigpen, C. H., & Cleckley, H. M. *The three faces of Eve.* New York: McGraw-Hill, 1957.

Thorndike, E. L. *Educational psychology,* 3 Vols. New York, 1913-1914.

Thurstone, L. L. A law of comparative judgment. *Psychological Review,* 1927, **34**, 273-286.

Thurstone, L. L. Attitudes can be measured. *American Journal of Sociology,* 1928, **33**, 529-554.

Thurstone, L. L. The Measurement of social attitudes. *Journal of Abnormal and Social Psychology,* 1931, **26**, 249-269.

Thurstone, L. L., & Chave, E. J. *The measurement of attitude.* Chicago: University of Chicago Press, 1929.

Torgerson, W. S. *Theory and methods of scaling.* New York: Wiley, 1958.

Torgerson, W. S. Multidimensional scaling of similarity. *Psychometrika,* 1965, **30**, 379-393.

Triandis, H. C., & Triandis, L. M. Some studies of social distance. In I. E. Steiner & M. Fishbein (Eds.), *Current studies in social psychology.* New York: Holt, Rinehart & Winston, 1965.

Tucker, L. R., & Messick, S. An individual differences model for multidimensional scaling. *Psychometrika,* 1963, **28**, 333-367.

Tversky, A. A general theory of polynomial conjoint measurement. *Journal of Mathematical Psychology,* 1967, **4**, 1-20.

Valins, S. Cognitive effects of false heart-rate feedback. *Journal of Personality and Social Psychology,* 1966, **4**, 400-408.

Wang, C. K. A. Suggested criteria for writing attitude statements. *Journal of Social Psychology,* 1932, **3**, 367-373.

Webb, E. J., Campbell, D. T., Schwartz, R. D., & Sechrest, L. *Unobtrusive measures: Nonreactive research in the social sciences.* Chicago: Rand McNally & Co., 1966.

Woodmansee, J. J. The pupil response as a measure of social attitudes. In G. F. Summers (Ed.), *Attitude measurement.* Chicago: Rand McNally & Co., 1970. Pp. 514-533.

Woodmansee, J. J., & Cook, S. W. Dimensions of verbal racial attitudes: Their identification and measurement. *Journal of Personality and Social Psychology,* 1967, **7**, 240-250.

Wrightsman, L. S. Wallace supporters and adherence to "law and order." *Journal of Personality and Social Psychology,* 1969, **13**, 17-22.

Name Index

Subject Index